George King

A Manual of Cinchona Cultivation in India

George King

A Manual of Cinchona Cultivation in India

ISBN/EAN: 9783337060206

Printed in Europe, USA, Canada, Australia, Japan

Cover: Foto ©Andreas Hilbeck / pixelio.de

More available books at **www.hansebooks.com**

A MANUAL

OF

CINCHONA CULTIVATION IN INDIA.

BY

GEORGE KING, M.B., F.L.S.,

SUPERINTENDENT OF THE ROYAL BOTANICAL GARDEN, CALCUTTA,
AND OF CINCHONA CULTIVATION IN BENGAL.

SECOND EDITION.

CALCUTTA:
OFFICE OF THE SUPERINTENDENT OF GOVERNMENT PRINTING.
1880.

CONTENTS.

		PAGE.
CHAPTER	I.—PRELIMINARY	1
„	II.—COLLECTION OF CINCHONA SEEDS IN SOUTH AMERICA	9
„	III.—INTRODUCTION INTO INDIA	16
„	IV.—CULTIVATION OF THE CINCHONA TREE. . . .	37
„	V.—CHEMISTRY OF THE BARK CROP	50
„	VI.—MODE OF HARVESTING THE BARK CROP . . .	58
„	VII.—ON THE LOCAL MANUFACTURE OF A CINCHONA FEBRIFUGE	69

APPENDIX A.—LIST OF THE CHIEF MODERN WORKS RELATING TO CINCHONA	79
„ B.—STATEMENT SHEWING THE QUANTITIES OF SULPHATE OF QUININE, CINCHONINE, CINCHONIDINE, AND QUINIDINE SUPPLIED TO THE INDIAN GOVERNMENT FROM 1867 TO 1873, WITH THE COST OF THE SAME	81
„ C.—STOCK OF TREES IN THE NILGIRI CINCHONA PLANTATIONS	84
„ D.—EXPENDITURE ON DITTO	87
„ E.—STOCK OF TREES IN THE SIKKIM CINCHONA PLANTATIONS	88
„ F.—EXPENDITURE AND REVENUE OF DITTO . . .	89
„ G.—PARTICULARS OF SOME OF THE SALES OF CINCHONA BARK HELD IN LONDON DURING 1875 AND PART OF 1876	ib.
„ H.—METEOROLOGY OF THE NILGIRI PLANTATIONS .	94
„ I & J.—METEOROLOGY OF THE SIKKIM PLANTATIONS .	97
„ K.—METEOROLOGY OF THE LANGDALE ESTATE, LINDULA DISTRICT, CEYLON	100
„ L.—TABLE OF PLANTING DISTANCES	101
„ M.—REPORTS ON THE ACTION OF THE MIXED CINCHONA ALKALOID ISSUED BY THE SIKKIM QUINOLOGIST .	ib.

CINCHONA CULTIVATION IN INDIA.

CHAPTER I.

PRELIMINARY.

OF the date and manner of the first discovery of the curative effects of Cinchona bark in malarious fevers we know nothing. And we are almost equally ignorant who the discoverers were, some writers claiming that merit for the aborigines of South America, while others assert, and with apparently greater accuracy, that not only did the Indians know nothing of the virtues of the bark until these were pointed out by their conquerors, the Spaniards, but that they still refuse to use bark as a febrifuge. The introduction of this medicine to Europe is associated with the Countess of Chinchon, wife of a Spanish Viceroy of Peru, who, having been cured by its use of an attack of fever contracted while in that country, brought a quantity of the bark to Europe on her return from South America, about the year 1639. Jesuit missionaries appear also to have taken an active part in its introduction. Hence the early names given to the medicine were Peruvian or Jesuit's Bark, and Countess's Powder. Nothing, however, was known to science of the tree producing this bark until 1739, when La Condamine and Jussieu, members of a French exploring expedition then in South America, obtained plants with the intention of sending them to the *Jardin des Plantes* at Paris; but the whole collection unfortunately perished in a storm at sea near the mouth of the River Amazon. The first living Cinchonas ever seen in Europe were some *Calisaya* plants raised at the *Jardin des Plantes* from seeds collected by Dr. Weddell, during his first journey to Bolivia in 1846. In 1742 Linnæus established the botanical genus Cinchona, a term which continues to be employed by the majority of botanists, although some writers prefer the name Chinchona, as more accurately perpetuating that of the noble lady who introduced this invaluable remedy to Europe.[1]

Discovery of therapeutic virtues of Peruvian bark.

Cinchona trees first known to science.

The number of species belonging to the genus Cinchona is reduced by Messrs. Hooker and Bentham in their *Genera Plantarum* to thirty-six. Many of these species are much given to variation or sporting, and a good many varieties, originating in this way, have been elevated to the rank of true species and described as such, much to the confusion of all interested in them. It would be entirely out of place to introduce here a botanical disquisition on the perplexing nomenclature of the plants belonging to this genus, and especially so as only about a dozen of the species yield bark of medicinal value, and of these but six are cultivated in India.

The various species of Cinchona.

---

[1] Mr. C. R. Markham, C.B., F.R.S., whose name is so intimately associated with the introduction of Cinchona into India, is a warm supporter of the spelling Chinchona. Mr. Markham has just published a biography of the Countess of Chinchon.

CINCHONA CULTIVATION IN INDIA.

The following table copied from the *Pharmacographia* of Messrs. species, together with their native countries and products :—

Conspectus of the Principal

Species (excluding sub-species and varieties) according to Weddell.	Where figured.	Native country.
I.—Stirps Cinchonæ officinalis—		
1 Cinchona officinalis, Hook.	Bot. Mag. 5364	Ecuador (Loxa)
2 „ macrocalyx, Pav.	Howard N. Q.	Peru
3 „ lucumæfolia, Pav.	Ditto	Ecuador, Peru
4 „ lanceolata, R. et P. (?)	Ditto	Peru
5 „ lancifolia, Mutis	Karst. tab. 11, 12	New Granada
6 „ amygdalifolia, Wedd.	Wedd. tab. 6	Peru, Bolivia
II.—Stirps Cinchonæ rugosæ—		
7 Cinchona Pitayensis, Wedd.	Karst. tab. 22 (*C. Trianæ*).	New Granada (*Popayan*).
8 „ rugosa, Pav.	Howard N. Q.	Peru
9 „ Mutisii, Lamb.	Ditto	Ecuador
10 „ hirsuta, R. et P.	Wedd. tab. 21	Peru
11 „ Carabayensis, Wed.	Wedd. tab. 19	Peru, Bolivia
12 „ Pahudiana, How.d	Howard N. Q.	Peru
13 „ asperifolia, Wedd.	Wedd. tab. 20	Bolivia
14 „ umbellulifera, Pav.	Howard N. Q.	Peru
15 „ glandulifera, R. et P.	Ditto	Peru
16 „ Humboldtiana, Lamb	Ditto	Peru
III.—Stirps Cinchonæ micranthæ—		
17 Cinchona australis, Wedd.	Wedd. tab. 8	South Bolivia
18 „ scrobiculata, H. et B.	Ditto	Peru
19 „ Peruviana, How.	Howard N. Q.	Peru
20 „ nitida, R. et P.	Ditto	Peru
21 „ micrantha, R. et P.	Ditto	Peru
IV.—Stirps Cinchonæ Calisayæ—		
22 Cinchona Calisaya, Wedd.	Wedd. tab. 9	Peru, Bolivia
23 „ elliptica, Wedd.	……	Peru (Carabaya)
V.—Stirps Cinchonæ ovatæ—		
24 Cinchona purpurea, R. et P.	Howard N. Q.	Peru (Huamalies)
25 „ rufinervis, Wedd.	Ditto	Peru, Bolivia
26 „ succirubra, Pav.	Ditto	Ecuador
27 „ ovata, R. et P.	Ditto	Peru, Bolivia
28 „ cordifolia, Mutis	Karst. tab. 8	New Granada, Peru.
29 „ Tucujensis, Karst.	Karst. tab. 9	Venezuela
30 „ pubescens, Vahl.	Wedd. tab. 16	Ecuador, Peru, Bolivia.
31 „ pupurascens, Wedd.	Wedd. tab. 18	Bolivia

PRELIMINARY.

Flückiger and Hanbury shews at a glance the names of the principal *Species of Cinchona.*

Where cultivated.	Produce.
India, Ceylon, Java.	Loxa or Crown Bark, Pale Bark.
......	Ashy Crown Bark. The sub-species *C. Palton* affords an important sort called *Palton Bark*, much used in the manufacture of quinine.
......	Carthagena Bark, confounded with Palton Bark, but is not so good.
India . .	Columbian Bark. Imported in immense quantities for manufacture of quinine. The soft Columbian Bark is produced by Howard's var. *oblonga.*
......	A poor bark, not now imported.
India . .	Pitayo bark. Very valuable; used by makers of quinine; it is the chief source of quinidine.
......	Bark unknown, probably valueless.
......	Bark not in commerce, contains only aricine.
......	Bark not collected.
India, Java .	A poor bark, yet of handsome appearance; propagation of tree discontinued.
......	Bark not collected.
......	Bark not known as a distinct sort.
......	Ditto ditto.
......	False Loxa bark; Jaen bark. A very bad bark.
....	An inferior bark, mixed with *Calisaya.* Bark formerly known as *Red Cusco Bark* or *Santa Ana Bark.*
India . . India . . India . .	} Grey Bark, Huanuco or Lima Bark. Chiefly consumed on the Continent.
India, Ceylon, Java, Jamaica, Mexico.	Calisaya Bark, Bolivian Bark, Yellow Bark. The tree exists under many varieties; bark also very variable.
......	Carabaya Bark. Bark scarcely now imported. *C. euneura*, Miq. (flower and fruit unknown), may perhaps be this species.
......	Huamalies Bark. Not now imported.
......	Bark a kind of light *Calisaya.*
India, Ceylon, Java, Jamaica.	Red Bark. Largely cultivated in British India.
India (?), Java (?)	Inferior brown and grey barks.
......	Columbian Bark (in part). Tree exists under many varieties; bark of some use in manufacture of quinine.
......	Maracaibo Bark.
......	Arica Bark (Cusco Bark from var. *Pelletieriana*). Some of the varieties contain aricine. *C. caloptera*, Miq., is probably a variety of this species.
......	Bark unknown in commerce.

The trees producing the medicinal barks are all natives of tropical
South America, where they are found in the
dense forests of the mountainous regions of the
western part of that continent at a height of from 2,500 to 9,000 feet
above the level of the sea, and in an equable, but comparatively cool
climate. The Cinchona-producing region forms a crescentic zone which
follows the contour of the coast-line, but nowhere actually touches it,
beginning at 10° N. and extending to 20° S. latitude. This crescentic
belt is nowhere much above a hundred miles in width, but its length
(following its curve) is more than two thousand. During its course it
passes through the territories of Venezuela,[1] New Granada, Ecuador,
Peru, and Bolivia. The Government of each of these countries has for
years derived more or less revenue from the duty levied on bark collected
within its limits and exported therefrom; but none of them, except the
last mentioned, has ever shewn any interest in the bark trade beyond
taxing it. Moreover, the more active interference shewn in Bolivia has
been quite as disastrous as the lazy *insouciance* of the more northern
states. These Governments proved, however, one and all, exceedingly
jealous of any attempt to procure for more civilised countries seeds or seedlings of the invaluable trees which they had done so little to conserve.

It must not be supposed that each of the medicinal species is to be
found growing throughout the whole length of the zone just described: on
the contrary, the distribution of the various species is very local, not only
as regards latitude, but as regards elevation above the sea. The species
found in the region between 10° N. and the equator (the barks of New
Granada) were described by Mutis in the last century and more recently
by Karsten in his *Flora Colombiæ*.[2] Mutis's notes remained in manu-
script until 1867, when Mr. Clements Markham succeeded in unearthing
and printing them, and both his notes and drawings have still more
recently been published at Paris by M. Triana in his *Nouvelles Etudes
sur les Quinquinas*. The Cinchonas of the region between the line and
14° S. (the barks of Ecuador and Northern Peru) were first examined
by Ruiz and Pavon, and a magnificent work founded on Pavon's specimens was published by Mr. J. E. Howard in 1862; while those indigenous in the region from the fourteenth parallel of south latitude to the
extremity of the zone in 20° south were described by M. Weddell in his
splendid monograph published at Paris in 1849.

The commercial Cinchona barks may be arranged as follows:—

I.—BARKS USED IN PHARMACY.[3]

(1.) *Pale Cinchona Bark, Loxa Bark or Crown Bark*—chiefly the produce of
Cinchona officinalis and imported from New Granada and Ecuador. This bark is
found only in the form of quills (*i. e.*, curled pieces derived from small stems or
branches). The pieces have a blackish brown or dark greyish external surface, vari-

---

[1] Bark from Venezuela has recently been introduced to the German market. Though poor in Quinine, it suitable for pharmaceutical purposes.
[2] For a list of modern works relating to Cinchona see Appendix A.
[3] For more complete details see the *Pharmacographia* (London, Macmillans, 1874) of Professor Flückiger and the late lamented Mr. Daniel Hanbury, a learned and elaborate work just published, and from which the following information concerning the commercial Cinchona barks has been condensed.

ously blotched with silver grey, and often beset with large and beautiful lichens. The surface of some of the quills is longitudinally wrinkled and moderately smooth, but in the majority it is distinctly marked with transverse cracks and is rough and harsh to the touch. The inner side is closely striated and of a bright yellowish brown. This bark breaks easily with a fracture which exhibits very short fibres in the inner side. It has a well-marked odour *sui generis* and an astringent bitter taste.

(2.) *Red Cinchona Bark*—the produce of *Cinchona succirubra* and imported from Ecuador. This bark occurs either in large flat-channelled pieces sometimes as much as half an inch in thickness, coated with their suberous envelope, which is rugged and warty. Its outermost layer in the young bark has a silvery appearance. The inner surface is close and fibrous and of a brick-red hue. The bark breaks with a short fibrous fracture.

(3.) *Yellow Cinchona Bark*.—This is the produce of *Cinchona calisaya* and is imported from Southern Peru and Bolivia. This bark is found in flat pieces and in quills.

Var. A: *Flat Calisaya Bark* is in irregular pieces a foot or more in length by 3 or 4 inches wide, but usually smaller, and $\frac{3}{10}$ths to $\frac{7}{10}$ths of an inch in thickness: devoid of suberous layer, consisting almost solely of liber, of uniform texture, compact and ponderous. Its colour is a rusty orange-brown, with darker stains on the outer surface. . . . The inner side has a wavy, close, fibrous texture. The bark breaks transversely with a fibrous fracture: the fibres of the broken ends are very short, easily detached, and with a lens are seen to be, many of them, faintly yellowish and translucent.

Var. B: *Quill Calisaya* is found in tubes $\frac{3}{4}$ths to $1\frac{1}{2}$ inch thick, often rolled up at both edges, thus forming double quills. They are always coated with a thick, rugged, corky layer, marked with deep longitudinal and transverse cracks, the edges of which are somewhat elevated. This suberous coat is silvery white or greyish, is easily detached, leaving its impression on the cinnamon-brown middle layer. The inner side is dark brown and finely fibrous. The transverse fracture is fibrous but very short. The same bark also occurs in quills of very small size and is then not distinguishable from Loxa bark.

II.—BARKS NOT USED IN PHARMACY.

These barks are exclusively used for making quinine. They are not used by druggists for the preparation of tinctures, decoctions, &c. In the market they are known as *Columbian*, *Carthagena*, or *Coqueta* Bark, and are produced by *Cinchona lancifolia* and *C. Pitayensis*. They are imported from New Granada. In appearance they vary much, but are generally orange-brown in colour. The *Pitayo* barks are usually imported in short flattish fragments or broken quills of brownish, rather than orange, colour, mostly covered with a dullish grey or internally reddish cork. The *Pitayo* barks are collected in the S. W. districts of *Columbia*.

Chemical composition of Cinchona barks.

The most important and at the same time peculiar constituents of Cinchona barks are the alkaloids enumerated in the following table [1] :—

Alkaloid.	Chemical composition.
Cinchonine	$C^{20} H^{24} N^2 O$
Cinchonidine (Quinidine of many writers)	same formula.
Quinine	$C^{20} H^{24} N^2 O^2$
Quinidine (Conquinine of Hesse)	same formula.
Quinamine	$C^{20} H^{26} N^2 O^2$

The alkaloids first separated.

There are other alkaloids, but they have no medicinal value so far as is yet known. These alkaloids exist in the bark in combination with certain organic acids called *Kinic*, *Cincho-tannic*, and *Quinovic*. Of the alkaloids above mentioned the most valued is undoubtedly *Quinine*. Although Cinchona barks have been employed in Europe as febrifuges

---

[1] *Pharmacographia*, p. 320.

for the past two centuries, it was not until the year 1820 that any of the several active principles to which they owe their efficacy was obtained in a separate form. The first to be so separated were Quinine and Cinchonine.[1] Quinidine[2] was discovered in 1833 and Cinchonidine[3] not until 1847. Quinamine was discovered so recently as 1872 by Hesse in bark of *C. succirubra* grown in Sikkim.

Soon after the discovery of Quinine, the sulphate of that alkaloid began to be used by the faculty as a medicine in cases where some preparation of "bark" was required, and gradually the new salt drove out of fashion to a very large extent the powder, tinctures, and decoctions of bark which formerly enjoyed such reputation in medical practice. Until the discovery of Quinidine and Cinchonidine, commercial Sulphate of Quinine consisted really of a mixture of the sulphates of all the Cinchona alkaloids, the outward appearance of these being alike. With the separation of the new alkaloids, chemical tests for their recognition began to be inserted in the various *Pharmacopæias*, and pure Quinine began to be insisted on in medical practice. The other alkaloids fell therefore into unmerited neglect, and they are still excluded from the British *Pharmacopæia*. Their admission to the category of officinal remedies can, however, only be a matter of time, as their excellence as febrifuges, as will be subsequently related, has now been thoroughly established by the trials given to them by officers of the medical services of the three Indian Presidencies. Cinchona bark still continues to be rated by the European Quinine-makers in proportion to the percentage of Quinine it contains, the other alkaloids being counted for little or nothing as marketable products. These unsaleable alkaloids have accordingly been accumulating in the hands of makers in Europe, and are or were recently purchaseable at a comparatively low price.[4] Regarding the proportion of these alkaloids in Cinchona bark, the learned authors of the *Pharmacographia*[5] write as follows :—

Proportion of alkaloids in Cinchona bark.

"This is liable to very great variation. We know from the experiments of Hesse (1871) that the bark of *C. pubescens*, Vahl., is sometimes devoid of alkaloid.[6] Similar observations made near Bogota upon *C. pitayensis*, Wedd., *C. corymbosa*, Karst., and *C. lancifolia*, Mutis, are due to Karsten. He ascertained[7] that barks of one district were sometimes devoid of Quinine, while those of the same species from a neighbouring locality yielded 3½ to 4½ per cent. of sulphate of quinine.

"Another striking example is furnished by De Vry[8] in his examination of quills of *C. officinalis* grown at Ootacamund, which he found to vary in percentage of alkaloids from 11·96 (of which 9·1 per cent. was Quinine) down to less than 1 per cent.

---

[1] Discovered by Pelletier and Caventou.
[2] Discovered by Henry and Delondre.
[3] Discovered by Winckler, who named it Quinidine.
[4] The following may be taken as approximates to the prices of the Cinchona alkaloids at the end of the year 1874: -

		s.	d.
Sulph. Quinine per ounce		9	0
,, Cinchonidine ,,		2	6
,, Cinchonine ,,		1	6
,, Quinidine ,,		0	4

[5] *Pharmacographia*, p. 324.
[6] *Berichte der Deutschen chem. Gesellsch.*, Berlin, 1871, p. 818.
[7] *Die med. Chinarinden Neu-Granada's*, 17, 20, 39.
[8] *Pharm. Journ.*, September 6th, 1873, 181.

PRELIMINARY. 7

"Among the innumerable published analyses of Cinchona bark, there are a great number shewing but a very small percentage of the useful principles, of which Quinine, the most valuable of all, is not seldom altogether wanting. The highest yield, on the other hand, hitherto observed, was obtained by Broughton,[1] from a bark grown at Ootacamund. This bark afforded not less than 13½ per cent. of alkaloids, among which Quinine was predominant.

"The few facts just mentioned shew that it is impossible to state even approximately any constant percentage of alkaloids in any given bark. We may, however, say that good Flat Calisaya Bark, as offered in the drug trade for pharmaceutical preparations, contains at least 5 to 6 per cent. of Quinine.

"As to *Crown* or *Loxa Bark*, the *cortex cinchonæ palidæ* of pharmacy, its merits are, to say the least, very uncertain. On its first introduction in the 17th century, when it was taken from the trunks and large branches of full-grown trees, it was doubtless an excellent medicinal bark; but the same cannot be said of much of that now found in commerce, which is to a large extent collected from very young wood.[2] Some of the Crown Bark produced in India is, however, of extraordinary excellency, as shewn by the recent experiments of De Vry.[3]

"As to *Red Bark*, the thick flat sort contains only 3 to 4 per cent. of alkaloids, but a large amount of colouring matter. The Quil Red Bark of the Indian plantations is a much better drug, some of it yielding 5 to 10 per cent. of alkaloids, more than a third of which is Quinine and a fourth Cinchonidine, the remainder being Cinchonine and Quinidine.

"The variation in the amount of alkaloids relates not merely to their total percentage, but also to the proportion which one bears to another. Quinine and Cinchonine are of the most frequent occurrence; Cinchonidine is less usual, while Quinidine is still less frequently met with and never in large amount. The experiments performed in India[4] have already shewn that external influences contribute in an important manner to the formation of this or that alkaloid; and it may even be hoped that the cultivators of Cinchona will discover methods of promoting the formation of Quinine, and of reducing, if not of excluding, that of the less valuable alkaloids."

Mode of collection of Cinchona barks.
The practice of the bark collectors in the wild regions in which Cinchonas naturally grow involved the destruction of each tree felled for its bark, yet no measures were ever taken by the owners of either public or private forests to secure supplies for the future by conservancy or replanting. Meanwhile the consumption of bark in Europe steadily increased, and, as a natural result, prices rose, and fears began to be entertained that the supply would ultimately fail. The British and Dutch Governments being, by reason of their tropical possessions, the largest consumers of Cinchona barks and of the alkaloids prepared from them,[5] their attention began to be seriously attracted to the increasing price and scarcity of the drug. So long ago as 1835, Dr. Forbes Royle, then Superintendent of the Botanical Garden at Saharunpore, suggested to the Indian Government that efforts should be made to introduce Cinchona on the Khasia and Nilgiri Hills. In 1847, and again in 1853 and 1856, he repeated his suggestion. In 1850 Dr. Grant, the Honourable East India Company's Apothecary General in Calcutta, urged this measure, and in 1852, Dr. Falconer, then Superin-

Fears entertained of failure of supply.

Introduction of Cinchona to India first suggested.

---
[1] Blue book—*East Indian Cinchona Plant*, 1870, 282; *Year book of Pharmacy*, 1871, 85.
[2] See *Howard's Analysis, and Observations*, Pharm. Journ., XIV (1855), 61—63.
[3] *Pharm. Journ.*, September 6, 1873, 184.
[4] Blue book, 1870, 116, 188, 205.
[5] For a statement of the quantity of Quinine purchased by the Indian Government from the year 1867 to 1872, see Appendix B.

tendent of the Calcutta Botanical Garden, recommended that an intelligent and qualified gardening collector should be deputed for a couple of years to the mountains of South America for the purpose of exploring the Cinchona forests and of procuring an ample stock of young plants and seeds of all the finest species. His proposals were, however, not approved of, and instead, an unsuccessful attempt was made to procure seeds through the agency of Her Majesty's Consuls on the west coast of South America. Three years after Dr. Falconer's suggestion had been made and disapproved, Dr. T. Thomson (his successor at the Calcutta Garden) again pressed the matter, as also did the late Dr. T. Anderson. The Medical Board supported the proposals of these officers in an elaborate minute. It was not, however, until 1858 that the despatch of a special agent to South America was sanctioned by the Secretary of State for India. Mr. Clements Markham, a gentleman who, besides a knowledge of Spanish and of the Quichua tongue,[1] possessed a knowledge of the country and people, volunteered to direct this arduous undertaking. In the meantime a few seeds of *Cinchona Calisaya* were got by Dr. Royle from Dr. Weddell, a surgeon who had accompanied a French expedition to South America, and who is the author of a valuable monograph of the medicinal Cinchonas. These seeds were sent to Calcutta, but failed to germinate. Plants were, however, raised from some of Dr. Weddell's seeds in the Botanical Gardens of Kew and Edinburgh, and six seedlings were entrusted to the care of Mr. Fortune (then on his way to China to obtain seeds and plants of the tea bush), by whom they were delivered to Dr. Falconer at the Botanical Gardens, Calcutta, in 1853. These were ultimately sent to Darjeeling; but only three of them arrived there alive, and these three also soon died.

Mr. C. R. Markham appointed to organise a Collecting Expedition.

---

[1] The language of the Indians of a district where some of the finest species of bark trees are indigenous.

CHAPTER II.

COLLECTION OF CINCHONA SEEDS IN SOUTH AMERICA.

The Dutch Collecting Expedition. IN 1852, the Minister for the Colonies of Holland proposed to the Government of the Hague that a properly qualified man should be sent to South America to collect Cinchona seeds and plants. Accordingly, M. Hasskarl, of the Botanical Garden of Buitenzorg in Java, was despatched on this mission. This gentleman arrived in Peru during the year 1853. After prolonged wanderings and exposure in the forests of Southern Peru, M. Hasskarl returned to the coast with a quantity of plants. These were sufficient to fill twenty Wardian cases, and, after a prosperous voyage, they were safely landed by him at Batavia in December 1854. M. Hasskarl had not the advantage of any local knowledge of the wild regions where he travelled, neither had he any acquaintance with the language of the natives. His avowed intention was chiefly to find seeds of *Calisaya*, but unfortunately he entered the Cinchona zone at a point where neither that, nor indeed any valuable species grows. He, however, collected the seeds of the species he found, imagining one of them to be true *Calisaya*. A portion of these seeds he sent by post to Holland, where some of them germinated, and the rest he despatched direct to Java. During his wanderings, M. Hasskarl did ultimately penetrate into a *Calisaya* region where he remained for a short time, but while there he appears to have trusted too implicitly to a native collector who led him to believe he was collecting the real *Calisaya*, while he was in fact gathering a worthless species. The twenty cases landed in Java by M. Hasskarl did not contain, it is believed, one plant of any valuable variety of *Calisaya*. A single plant of true *Calisaya* raised from some seeds brought to Paris by Dr. Weddell had, however, been sent to Java from the *Jardin des Plantes*, Paris, even prior to M. Hasskarl's appointment as collector. The *Cinchona introduced into Java.* Dutch experiment thus began with one plant of the best sort of Cinchona received from Paris, with a plentiful enough supply of doubtful species brought by M. Hasskarl, and with a quantity of seeds of the New Granada species (*lancifolia*), which had been sent by Dr. Karsten. This rather unfortunate beginning was followed by errors in cultivation, among which may be specially mentioned the method of sowing single seeds in separate bamboo pots, of planting out the seedlings, not in clear open ground, but under the shade and drip of the gigantic trees of the virgin forests of the mountains of Java, and finally of mistaking the worthless species brought by M. Hasskarl from Peru (and subsequently named *Pahudiana*) for a valuable Quinine-producing sort. At the end of the year 1860, the stock in the Java plantations consisted of nearly a million plants of *Cinchona Pahudiana*, with only about 7,000 of *Calisaya*. Having discovered the worthlessness of *Pahudiana*, the Dutch, in 1862, abandoned its cultivation. They also gave up (in 1864) the plan of planting out under forest shade. They have in recent years repeatedly got supplies of seed and plants of the best medicinal sorts from India and Ceylon, and their success of late has been great. According to the latest return (31st March 1875) there are in the Java plantations about two millions of Cinchonas of various ages. At least half of these are of undoubtedly valuable species, and amongst them are a hundred thousand of a variety of *Calisaya*, samples of the bark of some trees of which are said to have yielded on analysis the astonishing amount of from 10 to 13¼ per cent. of crystalline Sulphate of Quinine.[1]

The introduction of the medicinal Cinchonas into British India began under more favourable circumstances. Mr. Markham, having volunteered to direct the collection of seeds and seedlings in the Cinchona forests, organised a three-fold expedition, the sections of which began their explorations simultaneously early in 1860. Mr. Markham himself undertook to collect seeds of the *Calisaya* or Yellow Bark Tree (the most valuable of all the Cinchonas) in the forests of Bolivia and Southern Peru, where alone it is to be found. He arranged that Mr. Pritchett should explore the Grey Bark forests of Huanaco and Humalies in Central Peru, and that Messrs. Spruce and Cross should collect the seeds of the Red Bark tree on the eastern slopes of Chimborazo in the territory of Ecuador. Mr. Markham has narrated his adventures in an interesting volume,[2] in which he has besides collected much valuable information concerning the inhabitants and flora of regions he traversed. Landing at Islay in March 1860, Mr. Markham, accompanied by Mr. Weir (a practical gardener), proceeded inland in a north-easterly direction, crossed the two chains into which the Andes are there divided, and, after considerable hardship, arrived in one of the series of long valleys which stretch along the western slopes of the Snowy Range of Caravaya and descend to the great plain of Western Brazil. Mr. Markham penetrated this valley (called Tambopata) to a point beyond that reached by the distinguished French traveller, M. Weddell, and by the Dutch Agent, M. Hasskarl; and, notwithstanding that his proceedings were prematurely cut short by a failure in his food supplies, he was successful in collecting 497 plants of *Cinchona Calisaya* and 32 of the less valuable species, *ovata* and *micrantha*. The *Calisayas* were found chiefly to inhabit a belt of forest extending from 5,000 to 5,400 feet above the sea, while *micrantha* was found in a belt below, and the higher regions were occupied by *C. ovata*. The vegetation and soil of the region are thus described by Mr. Markham[3]:—

"This region is covered, with few exceptions, from the banks of the river to the summits of the mountain peaks, by a dense tropical forest. The formation is everywhere, as I have before said, an unfossiliferous, micaceous, slightly ferruginous,

---

[1] This wonderful variety of *Calisaya* having been originally raised from seeds collected by Mr. Ledger, has been called by the Dutch *C. Calisaya, variety Ledgeriana*.
[2] *Travels in Peru and India*, by Clements R. Markham, C.B., F.R.S., &c. London: John Murray, 1862.
[3] *Markham's Travels in Peru and India*, page 246.

metamorphic clay-slate, with veins of quartz, and the streams all contain more or less gold-dust. When exposed to the weather, this clay-slate quickly turns to a sticky yellow mud, and lower down it is very brittle, and easily breaks off in thin layers. The soil formed by the disintegration of the rock, mixed with decayed vegetable matter, is a heavy yellowish brown loam, but there is very little of it on the rocky sides of the ravine, and no depth of soil except on the few level spaces and gentle slopes near the banks of the river."

The finest trees were found in clear open spaces where they enjoyed plenty of light and air.

The half-caste collector who accompanied Mr. Markham distinguished three distinct varieties of true *Calisaya* which he named *fina* (= *C. Calisaya vera*), *morada* (=*C. Boliviana*), and *verde*. There is, besides these, the shrubby form which has a wider distribution and which is known locally as *ychu* and botanically as *Cinchona Calisaya*, variety *Josephiana*. The climate of this Tambopata valley (which lies

Its climate.

in the very centre of the *Calisaya* region) is wet and disagreeable. An intelligent settler gave Mr. Markham the following account of the seasons as regards rainfall[1]:—

"*January.*—Incessant rain, with damp heat day and night. Sun never seen. Fruits ripen.

"*February.*—Incessant rain and very hot Sun never seen. A coca harvest.

"*March.*—Less rain, hot days and nights, little sun. Bananas yield most during the rainy season.

"*April.*—Less rain, hot, humid nights, and little sun in the day-time.

"*May.*—A showery month, but little heavy rain. This is the month for planting coca and sugar-cane, and what is called the *michca*, or small sowing of maize, as well as yucas, aracachas, camotes, and other edible roots. Coffee harvest begins.

"*June.* –A dry hot month. Much sun and little rain. Coca harvest early in the month. Oranges and paccays ripen. Cool nights, but a fierce heat during the day.

"*July.*--The hottest and driest month, but with cool nights. Very few showers. Time for sowing gourds, pumpkins, and water-melons.

"*August.*—Generally dry. Trees begin to bud. A month for planting.

"*September.*—Rains begin. Time for blossoming of many trees. Coca harvest.

"*October.*—Rains increasing. Maize harvest, and time for the '*sambra grande*,' or great sowing of maize.

"*November.*—Heavy rains. A coca harvest.

"*December.*—Heavy rains. Pumpkins ripen."

Mr. Markham's observations[2] of the temperature of the Caravaya region extended over only the first fourteen days of May. They shew a mean temperature of $69\frac{5}{8}°$ Fahr. and a mean dew point of $61\frac{1}{4}°$. The highest temperature he observed was 75° and the lowest 56° Fahr. The mean minimum temperature at night he found to be $62\frac{5}{8}°$ Fahr. and the mean variation in 24 hours $10\frac{1}{8}°$ Fahr.

Appearance of *Calisaya* trees.

The tree *Calisayas* run up to a height of from 30 to 60 feet, and their stems have a girth equal to the body of a man, sometimes to that of two men. The shrubby variety runs from $6\frac{1}{2}$ to 12 feet in height. Both varieties flower in April and May; their blossoms are white, fringed, and very fragrant.

---

[1] *Markham's Travels in Peru and India*, pages 245 and 246.
[2] Ditto   ditto,   page 268.

On his return journey, Mr. Markham found the jealousy of the people aroused by rumours which had got abroad as to the nature of his mission. To return along the road he came by would have insured the destruction of his plants and possibly mischief to himself, so he had to resort to the stratagem of sending Mr. Weir back by the old route, and of himself proceeding with the plants in a straight line towards the coast through an unknown country and without a guide. After much hardship, he arrived in ten days at the town of Vilque with his plants in good order. A few more marches brought him to the port of Islay. Here, however, further difficulties awaited. The Custom House authorities, having discovered what the plant-cases contained, would not allow them to be shipped without an order from the Minister of Finance, which Mr. Markham had himself to go to Lima to procure. This caused a delay of three weeks. On the 24th June the cases were at last embarked on board a steamer bound for Panama, but not before a scheme had been set on foot by some patriotic Bolivian to kill the plants by pouring hot water on them through holes to be bored in the cases. Her Majesty's steamer *Vixen* was at this moment lying idle at Callao, and could have taken the plants straight to Madras with every chance of saving them all alive. Instead of this simple route being adopted, Mr. Markham was compelled by his orders to take his plants to India *vid* Panama, England, the Mediterranean and the Red Sea, and thus to expose them to transhipments and alterations of temperature which ultimately killed them all.

<small>Mr. Markham's return to the coast.</small>

About the time Mr. Markham was exploring the Yellow-Bark Forests of Southern Peru, Mr. Pritchett was collecting seeds and plants of the species producing Grey Bark in the forests near Huanaco in the northern part of the same territory, and was successful in bringing to Lima in the month of August a collection of seeds and half a mule-load of young plants of the three species, *micrantha, Peruviana,* and *nitida.* The two former are large trees with trunks often 70 feet in height and 30 inches in diameter. They grow at a height of from 4,000 to 7,000 feet above the sea, while *nitida* grows at a greater elevation and is a smaller tree.

<small>Mr. Pritchett's Collecting Expedition to Northern Peru.</small>

The task of collecting seeds and plants of the Red Bark had been undertaken by Mr. Spruce, a distinguished traveller and botanist who had been wandering in South America for some years prior to Mr. Markham's mission. Six months before Mr. Markham sailed from England, Mr. Spruce left his temporary home at Ambato in the Quitenian Andes to make a preliminary exploration of the forests where Red Bark trees were still to be found, and to ascertain at what season the seeds ripen. Having fixed on Limon as the most suitable head-quarters, he purchased from the owners of the forests (which in that region are private property) the right to collect seeds and plants. He further made an arrangement to accompany Dr. Taylor of Riobamba to Loxa, a town in the south of the Ecuador territory, for the purpose of procuring seeds of the Pale or Crown Bark. This latter arrangement was, however, frustrated by the prolonged and severe illness of Mr. Spruce. In July 1860, or nearly a year after his first start, Mr. Spruce was joined

<small>Messrs. Spruce and Cross's Red Bark Expedition.</small>

COLLECTION OF CINCHONA SEEDS IN SOUTH AMERICA. 13

at Limon by Mr. Cross, who had been sent out from England by Mr. Markham with Wardian cases to receive the plants that he and Mr. Spruce might succeed in collecting. Mr. Spruce having already thoroughly familiarised himself with the Red Bark forests, the work of collection was begun as soon as Mr. Cross arrived. Mr. Cross established a nursery at Limon, and there put in a number of cuttings of the Red Bark tree. He attended to these while Mr. Spruce searched for seeds. After spending about five months at Limon, Mr. Cross conveyed his rooted cuttings to the port of Guayaquil, and, thanks to his skill and excellent management, ultimately succeeded in taking them safely to India by the same route (but at a more favourable season) as Messrs. Markham and Pritchett's collections. Mr. Spruce's collections of seeds were sent to India by post.

Natural habitat of *Cinchona Succirubra*. Mr. Spruce describes the Red Bark forests as nearly exhausted. He met with only a few trees which had not been touched by bark-collectors; all the others which he saw consisted of shoots from the stumps of trees that had been felled. The Red Bark tree is naturally very handsome and attains a height of 50 feet. The climate of the country it inhabits is not so humid as that of the Caravaya and Huanaco forests where the Yellow and Gray Barks are found, and there is a distinct dry season extending from June to December. The following table,[1] compiled by Mr. Spruce, and founded on nearly a year's observation, gives some idea of the temperature:—

Mean minimum	61½° Fahr.	
Mean maximum	72¼ „	
Mean temperature at 6¼ P.M.	67¾ „	
Highest temperature observed	80½ „	on July 27th.
Lowest	57 „	11th.
Entire range	23½ „	
Mean daily variation	10¼ „	

Collection of seeds of Crown barks. After depositing his Red Bark plants in the Nilgiris early in 1861, Mr. Cross returned to South America and was commissioned to procure seeds of the Pale Barks in the forests near Loxa. These barks have a peculiar interest as being the first known in Europe. It was by the use of one of them that the Countess of Chinchon was cured, and it was on the flowers of one of the trees producing them that Linnæus founded his genus *Cinchona*. Mr. Cross started from Guayaquil in September 1861, and, after much hardship and exposure in the mountains near Loxa, he succeeded in returning to that port, after little more than two months' absence, with one hundred thousand seeds of *Cinchona Chahuarguera* and a smaller parcel of *Cinchona crispa*, both varieties of the Linnæan species *officinalis*. These seeds he forwarded to India by way of Southampton.

Habitats of the Crown bark. On arriving in South America, Mr. Cross found that, owing to the long-continued export of the Pale Barks of the Loxa country, but few trees remained in accessible places. In steep ravines and rocky gorges he succeeded, however, in finding a few mature trees. The soil of the

---

[1] *Markham's Travels in Peru and India*, page 321.

region he describes as fundamentally composed of decomposed micaceous schist and gneiss, but wherever Cinchona trees occurred, he found this to be covered by a layer of vegetable mould. *Cinchona officinalis* is a slender tree from 20 to 30 feet high, with a trunk from 8 to 10 inches in diameter at the base. Most of the plants he met with had been cut, but numerous shoots had grown from their stools. According to Mr. Cross's account, the climate is disagreeably moist. The rainy season begins in January and continues until May. June, July, and August are windy, with occasional heavy rain; the remainder of the year is fine, but showery. The temperature ranges from 34° to 70° Fahr., seldom falls below 40° and but rarely rises above 65°.

Collection of seeds of Pitayo barks.
Through a misunderstanding, a fine collection of *Pitayo* bark seeds made by Mr. Cross in 1863 was detained in South America until the vitality of most of the seeds had been impaired. These seeds, when ultimately sent to India, entirely failed to germinate. The valuable species yielding the Carthagena barks (*Cinchona lancifolia* and *Cinchona Pitayensis*) were therefore the last to be introduced into India. It was not indeed until 1868 that the same intrepid and skilful collector who had brought the Crown bark seeds was commissioned to undertake his third *Cinchona* expedition and to proceed to New Granada to collect seeds of these two sorts. Landing at the port of Buenaventura in the end of May of that year, Mr. Cross proceeded up the river Dagua as far as the village of Las Juntas, crossed the Western Cordillera and made his way up to Cauca village and thence to Pitayo, a hamlet standing nearly 9,000 feet above the sea level, in latitude 20° 30′ N. Here he collected a quantity of good seed. He found the trees growing, at elevations of from 7,300 to 9,800 feet, on slopes more or less steep, the surface soil of which was nearly pure vegetable mould, but very mealy and dry. The subsoils he found to be a yellow porous clay, in general loose and friable. Only a few Cinchona trees remained, and these were mostly small and mutilated. Mr. Cross's collections of seeds, numbering in all fifty-five packets, were despatched by post and reached the Nilgiris during the end of the year 1868. Mr. Cross's account of the climate of the Pitayo region shews it to be very damp, rain and mist being common during the greater part of the year. He says:—

"As[1] for New Granada, particularly the States of Cauca (in which Pitayo is situated) and Panama, no dry or summer wheather need be relied on or looked for at any time during the whole year. The cold climate of Ecuador is in general healthy, even where there is much rain with damp and fogs, whereas on the mountain slopes bordering on the Cauca Valley the inhabitants are often trembling with ague at an elevation of 7,500 feet above the level of the sea."

Mr. Cross gives no detailed meteorological observations in his report. His general account of the temperature of the Pitayo Quinine region is that "it ranges from 45° to 75° Fahr., but the general variable temperature of the Pinon is from 45° to 60° Fahr. He adds, "The climate indicated for Pitayo bark is exactly the same as that required for the Crown barks." During October Mr. Cross collected 270 plants. These were, after

---

[1] *Report on the Collections of Seeds and Plants of the Cinchonas of Pitayo*, by Robert Cross, London, 1871, page 31.

considerable trouble and hardship, landed at the coast in February 1869. There they were shipped, and a month later they were safely deposited at the Royal Gardens, Kew. In October following they were sent by overland route to India, and ultimately found a home—half on Nilgiris and half in the Sikkim Himalaya. Mr. Cross states that the Quinine trees of Pitayo are being rapidly extirpated. Writing in 1871, he says:—

"At present it is not possible to examine a developed healthy tree, as those from which I collected seeds were mere bushes, the natural habit of the plants having been much injured from barking or ill-treatment."

CHAPTER III.

INTRODUCTION INTO INDIA.

Introduction on the Nilgiris.

It had been previously settled that the Cinchona experiment in India should be begun in the Nilgri Hills, and on the recommendation of Dr. Cleghorn, then Conservator of Forests for Madras, and of Mr. McIvor, Superintendent of the Government Garden at Ootacamund, a patch of forest-land fifty acres in extent, situated behind the Government garden, was accordingly taken up and prepared for the first Cinchona experiment. Mr. Markham's consignment of *Calisaya* plants having reached England in a promising state, continued in that condition until they reached Alexandria. The passage through the Red Sea in the month of September and a week's unavoidable detention at Bombay, however, proved too great a trial for them, and on their arrival in the Nilgiris in October they were all in a dying state. Some cuttings were nevertheless made from them, but not one of these struck root. Mr. Pritchett's plants of Grey Bark were quite as unfortunate, for they reached India either dead or dying. Mr. Cross's plants of *succirubra* raised from cuttings at Limon, together with six *Calisayas* which had been raised at Kew in 1862, were the only living Cinchona plants collected by Mr. Markham's triple expedition that reached India in good condition. Mr. Cross deposited his plants in Mr. McIvor's hands at Ootacamund on 9th April 1861 in excellent order. The supplies of seeds procured by the three expeditions were more fortunate than the plants. These were sent in the first instance to the Royal Garden at Kew, where some were retained and sown. A few of the plants brought from South America were also retained at Kew, so that a sort of reserve depôt was formed there in case of failure in India. For the successful introduction of Cinchona into India and other British possessions, Government are largely indebted for advice, as well as for more active assistance, to Sir William and Dr. Joseph Hooker, the illustrious botanists, father and son, with whose names the fame of the great national institution at Kew has for half a century been identified.

The seeds not retained at Kew were sent to India: those of the Grey barks arrived in the Nilgiris in January 1861, and those of the Red barks two months later. In the month of December 1861 Dr. Anderson delivered over to Mr. McIvor at Ootacamund the plants he had brought from Java,[1] viz., 50 *Calisaya*, 4 *lancifolia*, and 284 *Pahudiana*. On the 4th March 1862, Mr. Cross's collection of Pale or Crown bark seeds from Loxa arrived, and the introduction of Cinchona to India became thus an accomplished fact.

Mr. Markham deputed to India to select sites for Cinchona.

It had been determined to take advantage of Mr. Markham's experience of the localities which form the natural home of the Cinchona by deputing him to choose suitable sites for its cultivation in India. Mr.

---

[1] A reference to Dr. Anderson's visit to Java will be found at page 24 of this report.

Markham accordingly arrived at Calicut in October 1860 (bringing his *Calisaya* plants with him), and for the next few months he was engaged in exploring the various hill ranges of Southern India with this object in view. The site selected by Dr. Cleghorn and Mr. McIvor at Ootacamund was approved of by Mr. Markham as resembling in its physical features and vegetation the natural habitats of *Calisaya* in the Caravaya forests. Planting in this site was greatly extended in subsequent years, and this tract of Cinchona is now known as the Dodabetta plantation. Mr. Markham examined the Nilgiri, Coorg, and Pulney hills, as also the Wynaad districts in the Madras Presidency and the Mahableshwar Hills in Bombay. He did not visit any part either of the Himalayas or of the Khasias, although both ranges had been suggested for Cinchona by Royle, Falconer, and others. Mr. Markham's opinion was that the Nilgiris offered decidedly the most suitable home for Cinchona, and on that range three sites were accordingly selected. The Dodabetta site was retained for the species affecting higher elevations and a cooler temperature, while for the more tropical species a lower site was chosen at a place called Neddiwattum, situated on the northern slope of the Nilgiris and on the cart-road from Ootacamund to the Malabar coast. Next to the Nilgiris Mr. Markham considered Coorg the most favourable district for Cinchona, and a spot near Mercara on the road to Mangalore was accordingly chosen for a plantation should it be found advisable to extend Government operations beyond the Nilgiris. The Pulneys were considered to afford a less suitable soil and climate, while the Mahableshwar climate, with its six months of incessant rain alternating with six of parching drought, was considered too extreme to offer much chance of success; the Mahableshwar soil was moreover found to be poor. The Anamallays, Shervaroys, and the hills near Courtallum were all considered too low. Of localities beyond Madras, Mr. Markham regarded Ceylon as the most promising, and after that island he believed Penang, the higher parts of Tenasserim, and the Khasia hills, likely to offer the most suitable sites for plantations.

The Dodabetta site on the Nilgiris.

The Dodabetta site is thus described by Mr. Markham[1]:—

"It is *shola*, or wooded ravine, at the back of the range of hills which rises behind the Government gardens, and which entirely protects it from the west winds; whilst another high ridge completely screens it from the east. It is 7,450 feet above the level of the sea, and from its sheltered position warmer by several degrees than Ootacamund. Like the thickets where the *Cinchona* grow on the pajonales of Caravaya in Peru, it is surrounded by steep grassy slopes, with a vegetation analogous to that of the Caravayan pajonales. Thus, the tree *Rhododendron* takes the place of the purple *Melastoma*, a large white lily that of the liliaceous sayri-sayri, while the *Gaultheriæ*, *Lycopodia*, and *Gallia* appear to be almost identical in the two regions. The vegetation of the interior of the ravine also resembles that of the pajonales of Sandia to some extent. It contains *Osbeckias*, Holly, Cinnamon, *Michelias*, *Vaccinium*, &c., with an undergrowth of *Lobelia*, *Acanthus*, and ferns, and species of Cinchonaceous shrubs. The temperature appears to be almost identical with that of the pejonales above the valley of Sandia in Peru, and the spot receives a moderate supply of rain and mist during both monsoons. It is true that this wooded ravine is more elevated, by nearly 1,500 feet, than any point in Caravaya where I found the

Vegetation and climate.

---

[1] Parliamentary Return, *East India* (*Cinchona Plant*), ordered by the House of Commons to be printed, 20th March 1863, page 132.

Cinchona growing; but Ootacamund is more than two degrees nearer the equator, and the temperature of the two places appears to be nearly the same. It is no small advantage, too, that the ravine is so near the Government gardens, and that the Cinchona plantation will thus have the benefit of Mr. McIvor's constant supervision."

The Neddiwattum site; its climate.

With regard to Neddiwattum Mr. Markham writes[1]:—

"The conditions most favourable for the production of Quinine in the bark of Cinchona plants are those of continuous vegetation, with a mean temperature of from 60° to 70° of Fahr., varying according to the species, an almost constant supply of moisture and an elevation of from 5,000 to 8,000 feet. In every part of the Western Ghâts the vegetation is subjected, during the last three months in the year, to an amount of dryness which is never known in the forests in South America, but I have seen no locality in India which more nearly meets the requirements of a Cinchona plantation than that which we selected on this occasion. It is, or was, within the Wynaad district, ... but it is in fact a portion of the northern slope of the Nilgiri Hills. The site is close to the travellers' bungalow at Neddiwattum, near the crest of the Ghât, on the road leading from Ootacamund to Manantoddy. The forest covers a declivitous slope, at an elevation of about 5,000 feet, and extends to the verge of the steep descent into the table-land of Wynaad. There is a good supply of water in the forest, and the soil is rich, its base being a mixture of syenite and laterite, curiously combined in strata. In this forest, amongst other plants, I found the *Hymenodictyon excelsum* (called by Roxburgh *Cinchona excelsa*, but excluded from the list of *Cinchona* by Weddell), an *Andromeda*, wild yam, cinnamon, pepper, coffee, wild ginger, an *Osbekia* with purple flowers, and numerous ferns and orchids. Moss in great quantities was hanging from the branches and trunks of the trees—a sure sign of great moisture. The jungle is within the narrow limits of the region which receives both the monsoons. Though protected, to some extent, from the south-west, it receives a full share of the monsoon during the summer, and is also refreshed by the north-east monsoon coming across Mysore from October to December. During the remaining months it is not without mists and heavy dues at night."

and vegetation.

The Pykara site.

Mailkoondah site.

In the end of the year 1862 a third plantation was opened out near Pykara waterfall on the northern side of the Nilgiris, and about a year later (in 1863) a fourth plantation was begun at a place called Mailkoodah on the Koondah Range, adjoining the Nilgiris. The sanction of the Secretary of State was also about this time given to the proposal to plant out 150 acres of Cinchona annually for ten years. This was, however, subsequently modified, and 1,200 acres were set down as the limit to which Government planting should be extended.

Vegetation of the Koondahs.

The Koondahs are described by Mr. Markham as the finest hills he had visited in India. He says[2]:—

"The forests cover their sides and crests, which bear more resemblance to the superb *montanas altas* of some parts of the Eastern Andes than to the scrubby *sholas* of the Nilgiris. The soil is of extraordinary depth and fertility, both in the forest and grass land, and there are abundant supplies of water. . . . . . The land reserved by Government is, I am fully convinced, the best site for a Cinchona plantation that has yet been selected, superior either to Dodabetta or Neddiwattum. The land is well protected from severe gales."

---

[1] Parliamentary Return, *East India (Cinchona Plant)*, ordered by the House of Commons to be printed, 20th March 1863, page 142.

[2] Parliamentary Return, *East India (Cinchona Plant)*, ordered by the House of Commons to be printed, 18th June 1866, page 221.

These advantages were, however, found to be counterbalanced by the distance of Mailkoondah from the station of Ootacamund and by its inaccessibility, no sufficient road having ever been made to it. The difficulties of getting and retaining labour sufficient to cultivate the plantation and of effective supervision were consequently found to be considerable. During 1872 it was therefore determined to abandon this plantation (an attempt to sell it having failed) and to leave the 75 acres of Cinchona trees which had been put out there to hold their own, as far as they can, against the indigenous vegetation, without help, and thus to form " a wild Cinchona wood." The expenditure on Mailkoondah up to the date of its abandonment had been Rs. 43,776.

Under Mr. McIvor's skilful management, the three plantations of Dodabetta, Neddiwattum, and Pykara continued steadily to prosper, and Mr. Markham, who re-visited the Nilgiris in 1865-66, considered the success that had been " attained in the short space of five years as quite astonishing."

Mr. McIvor's treatment[1] of the plants he had received was precisely that to which any experienced and skilful gardener would have submitted them. Little was known accurately of the exact conditions as to temperature and humidity which were likely to suit them best. Instead, therefore, of treating the living Cinchona plants entrusted to him in the open air, Mr. McIvor at once put them under the protection of glass, thus affording them an artificial climate which he could modify as to moisture and temperature in whatever way might appear desirable for their welfare.

Mr. McIvor's mode of treatment of Cinchona plants.

The seeds were, with equal judgment, sown in boxes filled with carefully prepared free, light, soil. As soon as the living Cinchonas which had been brought from South America had sufficiently recovered from the effects of their long journey, and the plants raised by him from the South American seeds had become large enough, Mr. McIvor began to propagate from them, at first by layers and afterwards by cuttings. The operation of layering so commonly employed in horticulture need not be described at length here. A peculiarity in Mr. McIvor's treatment was that, in order to absorb the moisture flowing from the wound, he put a small piece of dry brick under the cut when pegging the branch down into the soil. Propagation by cuttings and by leaf-buds was also pushed forward as rapidly as possible. All these operations were conducted with bottom heat,—that is to say, in soil brought to a comparatively high temperature by artificial means. When sufficiently large plants had been obtained, Mr. McIvor, after accustoming them to the temperature of the open air, planted out a number under different conditions, especially as to shade, with the view of discovering the best system of cultivation. It was found at the end of six months that plants which had been put out in the open without any shade, either artificial or natural, much surpassed in size and health others which had been planted out at the same time under the shade of forest trees. Mr. McIvor, therefore, decided to adopt the plan of planting in open cleared

---

[1] Mr. McIvor has himself described it in his notes on Cinchona cultivation—a little book published originally in 1863, and of which a second and enlarged edition appeared in 1865.

ground, instead of scattering his plants here and there, each in its own small clearing, in a virgin forest.

The Java mode of treatment. Several well-meant endeavours were at this time made by gentlemen who had visited the Dutch plantations in Java, to induce Government to sanction the adoption of the Dutch mode of cultivation in the Nilgiris in preference to that practised and advocated by Mr. McIvor. The Java plan of sowing seeds was as follows : Each seed was sown separately in a bamboo pot filled with rich soil. These pots consisted of joints of bamboo, the transverse partition of the joint serving as a bottom. These were arranged in the open air on long raised mounds of earth without any protection from rain. Prior to being sown, the seeds were steeped in water for twenty-four hours and, until they germinated, the soil in each pot was kept sufficiently moist by an occasional squeeze of a wet sponge. Such seeds as germinated yielded in about a year or eighteen months plants about a foot in height, and these were planted out in the forest in the sites they were intended permanently to occupy. These sites were well-dug circles of about six feet in diameter, "from the neighbourhood of which brushwood and overhanging trees had been cleared away, so as to admit the light perpendicularly while the side lights were somewhat excluded." The distance of these well-dug circles from each other was considerable, so that scattered over each acre of virgin forest there were only a few Cinchona plants. This was the system which it was proposed to substitute for the workmanlike plan adopted by Mr. McIvor. Fortunately, however, Mr. McIvor was allowed to follow the method of his own choosing—a method which was approved by the gentlemen who had seen Cinchona in its native forests, *viz.*, Messrs. Weddell, Markham, Cross, and Weir. Forty acres were, however, planted out in the Dutch mode; but of these, thirty were soon after cleared of their shade trees and converted into open plantations, leaving ten acres as a sufficient illustration of the disadvantages of the Java method. A few years later, the Dutch authorities themselves adopted the English practice and abandoned their own. Mr. McIvor was put in entire charge of the cultivation in the Nilgiris, and such was his success in propagation that on the 30th April 1862 (a little more than eighteen months after the beginning of the experiment) he was able to report the following stock of plants at Ootacamund, exclusive of two hundred and four that had been sent to Bengal:—

Red Barks (*C. succirubra*)	14,450
Yellow Barks (*C. Calisaya*)	237
Crown or Pale (*C. officinalis*) and its three varieties, Condaminea, Bonplandia, crispa } . . .	8,106
Pale Bark (*C. lancifolia*)	1
Grey Barks (*C. nitida, micrantha, Peruviana*)	8,276
The worthless species from Java (*C. Pahudiana*) . . .	425
Total	31,495

Species cultivated on the Nilgiris. Four months later, these numbers had been more than doubled. As has been stated, seeds or plants of all the valuable species of Cinchonas found in South America had been supplied to Mr. McIvor chiefly through the India Office and by the excellent arrangements of Mr. Markham. At the first start of the experiment on the Nilgiris the supply of *Calisaya* was very small. This was, however, amply compensated in 1865 by the offer of Mr. Money to exchange no less than thirteen pounds of seeds of the finest Bolivian varieties of this species which had been collected by Mr. Ledger, for a quantity of the Red Bark seed, which had by that time begun to be freely produced on the Nilgiri plantation. These thirteen pounds, on Mr. McIvor's lowest calculation of twenty thousand seeds to the ounce, should have yielded four millions of plants. Only sixty thousand plants were, however, raised, but these proved to be of three most excellent sorts. A plant of a very fine variety of Yellow Bark was also presented by Mr. J. E. Howard in 1867, and some supplies of seeds were likewise contributed by Mr. Markham. The cultivation of *Calisaya* has never, however, been very successful on the Nilgiris. In Mr. McIvor's words, "The habit of this species on the Nilgiris is less vigorous than the Red or Crown barks, the stems scarcely increasing more than half as much as these species in thickness during the same period of growth, and consequently as a bark-producing tree it is less valuable." Mr. McIvor also complains of the thinness of the bark. Mr. Broughton's report on the Nilgiri-grown *Calisaya* bark is, however, favourable. He found in 1870 that bark from comparatively young plants yielded about 4½ per cent. of medicinal alkaloids, of which nearly half was Quinine Sulphate. He accordingly recommended the extended cultivation of this species. This recommendation has, however, not hitherto been acted on. The cultivation of *C. succirubra* on the Nilgiris since Mr. Cross landed his collection of living plants there has been a steady success. The species is one very little liable to variation, and it is the hardiest and most easily propagated of all the medical Cinchonas. Mr. Cross' original collections of seed of the Pale barks had germinated so well at Ootacamund that little was left to be done subsequently in the way of adding new varieties of this sort. Mr. Howard, however, sent a plant of *uritusinga* to Mr. McIvor, from which a stock of that variety was ultimately obtained. Of the fifty-five packets of seed of Pitayo barks sent from New Granada by Mr. Cross, forty-seven packets arrived at Ootacamund during the years 1868 and 1869, but they yielded in all only eighty-six plants. This result is attributable to their mouldy condition on arrival. Mr. Cross's consignment of living plants of *Cinchona Pitayensis*, after having been nurtured at Kew for more than six months, was taken to India under the charge of Dr. B. Simpson, of the Bengal Medical Service, and deposited by him, half on the Nilgiris and half in Sikkim. The Nilgiri consignment reached Ootacamund in the end of 1869. The plants have since been slightly increased in number.

During the year 1868, the attention of Mr. Broughton was first attracted by a few plants in the Pale bark plantation at Dodabetta which differed from their neighbours by having narrower leaves. On analysis, the bark of this variety was found to yield the unprecedented amount of from 7 to 10 per cent. of crystalline *quinine*, the total alkaloid in the bark being more than 11 per cent. Provisionally christened *Cinchona mirabilis* from this circumstance, the specific name of this variety has been changed into *angustifolia*.

Discovery of Cinchona mirabilis or angustifolia.

Extension of Nilgiri plantations discontinued in 1869-70.

The limit of twelve hundred acres fixed for the Nilgiri plantations having been reached during the official year 1869-70, propagation and planting on the scale hitherto followed became no longer necessary, and the establishments on all three plantations were considerably reduced. Any extension which has since taken place has been entirely of the new and valuable sorts more recently received, *viz.*, *Calisaya Pitayensis*, and the wonderfully rich *angustifolia* discovered by Mr. Broughton at Dodabetta. From an early period in their history and until 1869, the Nilgiri plantations were largely worked by convict labour, and jails were erected at Neddiwattum and Dodabetta for the accommodation of the prisoners. This arrangement appears to have worked satisfactorily. Since the end of the official year 1868-69, the labour has been of the ordinary sort. The distribution of Cinchona seeds and plants to private persons has all along been a prominent feature in the operations of these plantations. At first, so high a price as [1] four annas was charged for each plant; this was subsequently reduced to one anna, and more recently to two pies. For public purposes plants have of late been given gratuitously. The total number of plants distributed up to 31st January 1875 is 235,747. The Red bark trees began to yield seed in 1866, and the other species followed soon after. Up to the date just quoted, thirty pounds of Cinchona seed of sorts had been distributed gratuitously. With the view of recouping Government for the past expenditure on Cinchona and of reducing the annual outlay for the future, it was decided early in 1871 to sell the Pykara and Mailkoonda plantations. As already mentioned, no one would buy the latter, and it was consequently abandoned. An offer to lease Pykara was, however, made, but being considered unsatisfactory, was declined, and the plantation is still worked by Government.

Present stock on the Nilgiris.

At the end of the official year 1873-74, the total number of trees in permanent plantations in the Nilgiris stood as follows [2]:—

				Acreage.	
				Surface.	Base.
Total of plants of all sorts on Neddiwattum			474,740	455	371·24
,, ,, ,, Dodabetta			345,980	378	287·25
,, ,, ,, Pykara			304,484	336	243·00
			1,125,204	1,169	901·49
Mailkoonda (abandoned)			65,254	75	40·28
Total			1,190,458	1,244	941·77

This gives an average of about 1,042 trees per acre for Neddiwattum, 915 per acre for Dodabetta, and 906 per acre for Pykara. The trees are not, however, equidistant in all parts of these plantations, for some of the older trees stand 12 × 12 feet apart, and a small number so close as 3 × 3 feet.

---

[1] The equivalents of these sums in English money are, respectively, sixpence, three half-pence, and a farthing.
[2] For minuter details see Appendix C.

The cost of these plantations to the same date has been a follows¹:—

General charges—	Rs.
For Direction, Offices, and Propagation	1,61,172
Special charges—	
Expenditure at Neddiwattum	2,36,239
Dodabetta	1,52,318
Pykara	81,501
	6,03,059
At Mailkoonda (abandoned)	43,776
Total to 31st March 1873	6,75,026

This gives an average, excluding Mailkoonda entirely, of about Rs. 542 per surface acre, and 8 annas 9 pies (or one shilling and a penny) a tree. It is important to note that for years convict labour was largely used on the plantation. On the other hand, the revenue received from the plantation since its commencement to the end of the official year 1868-69 has been as follows ²:—

			Rs.
Sale of plants in	1863-64		5,100
"	"	1864-65	4,809
"	"	1866-67	2,450
"	"	1868-69	1,680

Introduction in Bengal.

Cinchona cultivation in the Bengal Presidency began under less favourable circumstances than in Madras. No plants were sent hither from South America, nor was the experience of Mr. Markham available in the selection of the most hopeful localities in the Himalayas or Khasias. From its commencement, and until his departure from India in 1869, the superintendence of the Cinchona experiment in Bengal was under the direction of Dr. Thomas Anderson, Superintendent of the Royal Botanical Garden, Calcutta. Exposure in the feverish regions of the outer Himalaya, together with almost daily subjection, for weeks on end, to the sudden changes of temperature incident on passing from the cold climate of Darjeeling, where he lived, to the hot steamy valleys of the Cinchona reserve, then a houseless waste, laid the seeds of disease of the liver which caused the premature death during 1870 of this able and zealous servant of Government. Subsequently to 1869 it has been under the direction of Dr. Anderson's successors. Since 1866, the Sikkim plantations have been under the executive charge of Mr. J. Gammie, the resident manager, and to him their success has been largely due. The first Cinchona seeds received by Dr. Anderson were some sent by Sir W. J. Hooker to the Botanical Gardens, Calcutta, in 1861. In December of that year these had produced thirty-one plants. During the same year the Government of Bengal and the Supreme Government

---

¹ See Appendix D for fuller details. This is exclusive of all charges connected with Mr. Broughton. His pay as Quinologist and the expenditure on his analytical laboratory and factory have been quite distinct from the plantation accounts. The Sikkim charges given in Appendix F include, on the other hand, not only the cost of plantation, but also that of the Quinologist's laboratory and factory as well.
² Accountant-General's letter, dated 19th January 1870.

of India had taken up the matter in earnest, and accordingly, in the month of September, Dr. Anderson was sent to Java with the double object of familiarising himself with the Dutch mode of cultivation and of conveying to India the plants which the Governor of that colony had generously offered to the Government of India. Dr. Anderson returned from Java in November, bringing with him 412 living Cinchona plants and a quantity of seeds of *C. Pahudiana*. Shortly after his return from Java, Dr. Anderson proceeded to Ootacamund, and there made over to Mr. McIvor 50 of the *Calisaya*, 284 of the *Pahudiana*, and 4 of the *lancifolia* plants which he had brought from Java. In return he took to Calcutta from Ootacamund 193 plants of *succirubra* and of the species yielding Grey bark. Some of the Java plants died in Calcutta, and on the 19th January 1862 the total stock of plants in the Botanical Gardens there from all sources consisted of 289 plants. Dr. Anderson recommended that these should be sent to Sikkim, that being the part of the Himalaya which offered, in his opinion, the greatest hope of success. Government sanctioned this proposal, and in March of the same year Dr. Anderson proceeded to Darjeeling, accompanied by a gardener in charge of the plants 249. The conduct of the Sikkim experiment in its earlier stages was influenced by the error of over-estimating the amount of coolness and moisture required for Cinchonas. The accounts of the explorers of Cinchona forests (founded of course on imperfect experience) on the whole rather countenanced the notion that all the species except *Calisaya* thrive best in regions where, in the scanty intervals between the showers, there is more mist than sunshine. A wearied collector who had spent the day in climbing rugged hill-sides under a hot sun in search of Cinchona trees, shivering at night in an open shanty high on the Andes, was naturally inclined to consider as extremely cold a night-temperature which a thermometer shewed to have been only about 40° Fahr., and such impressions formed a large part of the information which the introducers of Cinchona into India had to guide them in choosing sites for plantations. With the view of finding for them as wet, chilly, and disagreeable a climate as possible, Dr. Anderson chose a spot near the summit of Sinchul, a mountain of the outer range of the Sikkim Himalaya, which rises to an elevation above the sea of nearly 9,000 feet and thus intercepts a large share of the clouds passing northwards from the plains. A conservatory was quickly extemporised there by adapting an empty house to the purpose, and a propagating pit was soon built, in which the plants, now reduced in number to 211, were placed on the first day of June 1862. Under the care of Mr. Jaffrey, these were rapidly increased during the succeeding five months. The winter climate of Sinchul proved, however, by far too severe for Cinchonas. Most of the land in the Darjeeling district having been previously taken up by private speculators for tea cultivation, it was difficult for Dr. Anderson to find any suitable locality for a Cinchona plantation. After much search, however, he succeeded in hiring for a nursery, a house and garden at Lebong, a warm, well-sheltered spur below Darjeeling, and 6,000 feet above the level of the sea. The Sinchul stock, amounting to 2,484 plants (chiefly *Pahudiana*, but including 30 Pale barks derived from Ceylon seeds and also some *succirubra* and *Calisaya*), was accordingly removed there on 1st April 1863. These were supplemented by 97 *succirubras*, 21 *Calisayas*, 94 *officinalis*, and 115 Grey barks received from Madras about the same time. For the formation of a permanent plantation, Dr. Anderson had to be content with land in the then densely forest-clad and little-known valley of the Rungbee, twelve miles distant from Darjeeling, and at that time unconnected with that station by any road. Dr. Anderson's early difficulties are well described in his own words:—

<small>Rungbee plantation begun.</small>

"I laboured," he writes in 1863, "under the disadvantage last year[1] of being quite ignorant of the nature of the country of British Sikkim beyond what I could learn from the accounts of Dr. Hooker, as well as from the collections of dry plants from Sikkim which exist in the Calcutta herbarium. I had formed very inadequate ideas of the difficulty of reaching Darjeeling, of the condition of the roads leading to it, and of the resources of the station as regards labour, especially such skilled labour as I required, such as native gardeners, carpenters, and masons. I also supposed that no difficulty would be experienced in obtaining abundance of land, the property of Government, in the neighbourhood of Darjeeling, that glass for the conservatory, and flowerpots, &c., could be procured in Darjeeling. Some idea, however, will be obtained of the difficulties with which the experiment had to contend when I state that no suitable Government land could be got nearer than twelve miles from the station, and that, to reach this spot, an almost impenetrable forest had to be passed through, requiring every step to be cleared by Lepchas with their long knives. On leaving Calcutta, I had hoped that the permanent propagating houses, the gardener's house, and huts for the coolies, would have been finished in three months; instead of which, it soon appeared that until a bridle path, eight miles long, could be finished, the buildings could not even be commenced, and that, instead of three months being required to complete them, two years was the shortest time in which they could be ready. No temporary buildings could be obtained either, except barracks on the windy and cold crest of Sinchul, 8,600 feet above the sea. Before these could be converted into a conservatory, glass had to be procured from Calcutta, 400 miles distant. The manufactory of flowerpots was also unknown at Darjeeling, and so even they had to be obtained from Calcutta. Then, no labour of any kind could be got to supply the place of the two Bengalee gardeners, who insisted on returning to Calcutta within three months of their arrival at Darjeeling; and the European gardener had therefore to perform all the operations of the simplest kind with his own hand, and this is still the case. Such an apparently easily procurable substance as white river-sand could not be got in Sikkim,—not that none existed there, but that, during the rains, the courses of the rivers were so full of water that the beds of sand were all concealed. Accordingly, a maund of sand was sent for from the Botanic Gardens in Calcutta. No packages of any kind ever reached Darjeeling from Calcutta in less than six weeks, the usual time occupied in the transit being two months. It will thus be seen that the commencement of Cinchona cultivation in Sikkim entailed a great many preliminary operations before the propagation of plants could be attempted; and it is only now with tools, flowerpots, bell-glasses, and hand-frames received from Calcutta, and a determination to be contented with such means as are procurable in Darjeeling, that the success I have been able to report has been obtained."

<small>Early difficulties.</small>

It was found necessary to continue the nursery at Lebong until April 1865 and to open another at Rungyroon, a spot half-way between Darjeeling and the future plantation at Rungbee, the Rungyroon location

---

[1] Parliamentary Return, *East India* (*Cinchona Plant*), ordered by the House of Commons to be printed, 8th June 1866, page 298.

being especially adapted for a distribution nursery. Ground was broken in the Rungbee Valley, in June 1864, at a spot 4,410 feet above the sea level, on the south-eastern slope of a long spur running out from the main ridge of Sinchul. The elevation of the lower part of this spur is about 1,300 feet. Below 4,000 feet, the land in the valley had been previously cleared for native cultivation of Indian corn and millet. Higher up, the spur was (and still remains) covered with a virgin forest of tall trees, the stems of which are clothed with moss, ferns, epiphytal orchids, aroids, and *Begonias*. The undergrowth consists of ferns, *Acanthaceæ*, and other shrubs, especially prominent among the latter being several species of shade-loving *Cinchonaceæ*. In the wetter places are patches of wild plantain, and here and there occur impenetrable cane-brakes. The first and only piece of planting done during the year 1864 was a patch containing the following :—

Species cultivated at Rungbee.

	Plants.
Cinchona succirubra	100
,, *officinalis*	100
,, *micrantha*	50
,, *Calisaya*	2
,, *Pahudiana*	271
Total Plants	523

At this time the out-door plantations on the Nilgiris contained 165,351 plants. Two hundred seeds of *C. Calisaya* of Weddell's stock were received from Java during this year, but of these only nine germinated. Some seed of *C. Pitayensis*, received from South America through Mr. Markham, entirely failed. On the abandonment of the nursery at Lebong all the stock of plants was removed to Rungbee, which henceforth became the head-quarters of the cultivation, and four fresh spots were opened there at various elevations with the view of discovering a suitable home for each species. One plantation was formed at 5,321 feet above the sea; others at 5,000, 3,332 and 2,556 feet respectively, and towards the end of the year 1865 a small plantation was formed as an experiment in the Teesta Valley, in an open Sâl forest, at an elevation of only 1,000 feet above the sea, and in a locality of which the climate differs considerably from that of any part of the Rungbee Valley. During the official year 1865-66 nearly 6,000 plants were put out in permanent plantation, and the total stock of all sorts and ages amounted at the end of that year to 178,741. At the same date the Nilgiri plantations contained about a million and a half plants of all ages, of which 40,000 were in permanent plantations.

Propagation by cuttings of *C. succirubra* and *C. officinalis* went on vigorously during succeeding years. It gradually, however, became apparent that *officinalis* does not thrive in Sikkim, and, after about 400,000 plants had been put out, all further planting of this species was discontinued, and not only so, but three-fourths of the area covered by it were replanted with *succirubra*. Only 125,000 plants of *officinalis* are therefore now returned. Of *C. succirubra* there were on 1st April 1875, 2,390,000 trees. The propagation of this species is now thoroughly understood and can be carried on with ease to any extent that may be considered desirable. The best of all the medicinal Cinchonas—

namely, *Calisaya* or Yellow bark—promises to do well in Sikkim, and there were in the plantation on 1st April 1875, 354,500 trees of that species, besides young plants in the nurseries. The great preponderance of *succirubra* trees in the plantation is not due to a preference for that species over *Calisaya*, but to the fact that the Red bark tree is hardier, much more easily propagated, and has a much wider range as regards conditions of growth than *Calisaya*. Owing to the backwardness of *Calisaya* to yield seed, propagation by artificial methods had to be relied on until 1874. During that year the *Calisaya* trees for the first time seeded freely; it was therefore hoped that rapid extension of this species by seedlings could then be begun. In the meantime Mr. Wood, the recently-appointed Quinologist, had analysed the bark of the numerous varieties[1] of this species which occur on the plantation, and had pointed out that whereas certain of these varieties yield a bark containing as much as $7\frac{1}{2}$ per cent. of total alkaloid, of which nearly the whole is Quinine, others yield so little as $1\frac{1}{2}$ per cent. of total alkaloid. The best varieties (yielding from $5\frac{1}{4}$ to $7\frac{1}{2}$ per cent. of total alkaloid) are all characterised by narrow leaves (in one of them these are purple below), perfectly white flowers and small seed-vessels. The bad varieties, on the other hand, have large broad leaves, purplish flowers, and large seed-vessels.

Although seed was saved from the fine varieties only, so large a proportion of the resulting seedlings shewed such a marked resemblance to the bad varieties that it was resolved to plant out none of them, and to trust to propagation by cuttings for any further extensions which may be decided upon. Of other species originally introduced into Sikkim, one—namely, *C. Pahudiana*—proved worthless, and its cultivation has long since been entirely abandoned. The Grey barks (*C. micrantha, C. Peruviana, C. nitida*) being poor in Quinine, the cultivation of these species is now no longer carried on. *C. Pitayensis* is closely allied in nature to *officinalis*, and apparently will not succeed in Sikkim. One important species is now receiving special attention. This was referred to in the earlier reports on the Sikkim plantation as a hybrid. The first plant of this appeared amongst a set of seedlings raised from seed got some years ago from Dr. Thwaites, F.R.S., Director of the Royal Botanical Gardens, Ceylon. It is possible that this may turn out to be a distinct species and not a hybrid. Analysis of its bark shews it to contain much Quinine. Since the discovery of this fact every effort has been made to propagate this variety. Experience, moreover, proves

---

[1] Mr. Wood's analysis of six varieties of Sikkim *Calisaya* is contained in the following table, extracted from his report to the Government of Bengal, dated 5th August 1874. The variety marked No. 1 in the table may be taken as a fair example of the bad varieties, which number about half a dozen.

Cinchona Calisaya varieties.	1	2	3	4	5	6
Total alkaloid	1·6	6·1	5·57	7·1	5·75	7·4
Alkaloid sol. in Ether	0·82	5·9	5·21	6·93	5·75	7·4
Cryst. Sulphate of Quinine	None.	4·53	4·6	6·92	5·34	6·2

that it grows well in Sikkim and at a higher level than *Calisaya*. Of this variety 21,000 plants were in permanent cultivation on 1st April 1875. Like *Calisaya*, this variety does not come true to seed, a large majority of its seedlings closely resembling *C. officinalis* in appearance. It must therefore be propagated by cuttings in the manner to be described hereafter. A form similar to this sprung up accidentally in some of the Nilgiri plantations, but does not appear to have been propagated to any extent on those belonging to Government.

The details of the Sikkim plantations, as they stood on the 1st April 1875, will be found in Appendix E of this report. The total expenditure on the Sikkim plantations to the date just mentioned, including all quinological charges, has been Rs. 6,46,243. The total revenue to the same date amounts to Rs. 7,958,[1] but the plantation has not as yet begun to be worked for revenue.

A Cinchona plantation was begun by a private company in Sikkim almost simultaneously with that belonging to Government. Patches of Cinchona were also planted in several tea gardens in the district, but the cultivation has not commended itself to private enterprise to the same extent in Sikkim as in the Nilgiris.

Introduction in other parts of India.
Encouraged by its success on the Nilgiris, Cinchona cultivation was warmly taken up by European residents in the other high lands and hill ranges of the Madras Presidency. The coffee planters of Wynaad put out a good many Red bark trees on their estates. These are found to grow well: their bark, however, in common with that grown at low elevations elsewhere, is comparatively poor in alkaloid, and the results on the whole are not very encouraging.

In the Wynaad district.

In South Canara.
In South Canara a small plantation was formed in 1869 at a place called Nagooli above the Koloor Ghât and at an elevation of 2,500 feet above the sea, but the experiment there was pronounced by the Madras Government as unlikely to be productive of useful results, and has therefore been practically abandoned.

In Ganjam.
On the Mahendra Mountain in the Ganjam district, the opening of a small plantation was sanctioned by the Madras Government early in 1871.

In the Nulla Mully Hills.
Under the Forest Department an attempt was made to introduce Cinchona on the Nulla Mully hills, but the first hot weather killed all the plants (Red barks), and, a similar fate overtaking a second supply planted in 1867, the experiment was abandoned. As the highest peak of the Nulla Mullys rises to only 3,300 feet, and the whole range is exposed to hot winds for two or three months of the year, the result is scarcely to be wondered at.

In Coorg.
The following account of Cinchona cultivation in Coorg has been furnished by order of the Chief Commissioner:—

"With the object of introducing the experimental cultivation of Cinchona into Coorg, a piece of ground about an acre in extent was taken up in 1863 by the district

---

[1] See Appendix F.

officer, and placed under the charge of the Reverend Mr. Richter, the Principal of the Central School. In 1872 the ground was enlarged by adding to it a neglected coffee garden of about seven acres in extent, and, besides the cultivation of the Cinchona plant, an effort was made to introduce and acclimatise fruit and other useful trees.

"The number of Cinchona trees within the limits of the original plantation is now about 412, of which 323 are from three to ten years old. Their condition is stated to be satisfactory, though there have been several casualties from dry rot.

"From the nursery attached to the garden some of the coffee planters and ryots of the district have obtained seedlings, and the cultivation has, it is stated, become somewhat extended.

Total Alkaloids	0·23
Quinine	1·04
Cinchonine and Cinchonidine	5·10
Crystallized Sulphates of Quinine obtained	0·63
Cinchonidine	5·11
Total Crystallized Sulphates obtained	5·74

"In 1870 some of the bark from the Government trees was sent to Mr. Broughton, the Quinologist, for analysis. His report shews the results marginally noted. The bark Mr. Broughton pronounced of good appearance and apparently in a well-prepared state.

"The cost of establishment was for the first ten years at the rate of only Rs. 6 per mensem, but when the plantation was enlarged the expenditure increased, and from September 1873 to July 1874, Rs. 235 were spent in clearing the old jungle, cutting a new road, and forming a nursery, as well as effecting other improvements. Mr. Richter's own labours are gratuitous.

"The Mysore Government is not fully satisfied that the maintenance of this garden is justified by the results that have been obtained, and the Superintendent of Coorg has been directed to report more fully on the subject."

The average girth and height of the trees in June 1875 was as follows:—

Age of trees.	Average girth.	Average height.
12 years.	28 inches.	39 feet.
10 ,,	21 ,,	30 ,,
6 ,,	13 ,,	17 ,,
4 ,,	9 ,,	9 ,,

In Travancore,

The Travancore Government, by the advice of the Resident, Mr. Maltby, opened in 1862 a plantation of Cinchona at Peermede, near the station of Maryville, a promising locality on the Travancore portion of the Western Ghâts and elevated about 3,000 feet above the sea. This locality was visited in 1865 by Mr. Markham and Dr. Cleghorn, then Conservator of Forests for Madras, and was approved of as likely to suit Cinchona. In 1869 the plantation contained 3,552 trees, chiefly Red bark, and in 1870 these were reported by the Resident at the Travancore Court as "looking generally very well." Shortly after this, they were visited and reported upon by Mr. McIvor, whose verdict was that the trees were cankered. The existence, however, of a certain amount of disease, of the nature of canker, is one of the accidents of Cinchona cultivation in all parts of India, and its occurrence need not be regarded as necessarily proving the unsuitability of any particular locality for Cinchona cultivation.

In the Pulney Hills.

In the Pulney Hills the introduction of Cinchona has received some attention both from Government officials and from private parties, notably from the Roman Catholic missionaries. Planting has not been pursued on any large scale, but it has been tried at several places. The experience is that the trees grow fairly, but that the bark is not very rich in alkaloids. In October 1872 there were 700 healthy Cinchona trees in the Mission House garden at Kodicanal.

In the Tinnivelly Hills experimental plantations were made at various elevations from about 2,700 to 4,300 feet, and under various conditions of exposure and soil. Some trees were planted on virgin forest land cleared for the purpose, others were put in grass-land. At one of the spots near Papanassam (3,000 feet) 32 *succirubra* trees and 98 of *officinalis* were planted in September 1866. Three years later, 30 of the former and 70 of the latter were in good condition, the tallest of them having reached a height of 13 feet, and the average height of the whole being 8 to 10 feet. When it is stated that these trees had neither been planted nor tended by skilled labour, but had been under the care of wild hill-men, this result is very favourable. The portion of the Tinnivelly Hills where the plantations are situated being practically uninhabited, the experiment cannot be said to have had the amount of attention that it merits.

In the Tinnivelly Hills.

On the Shevaroy range *Cinchona succirubra* seems to thrive. A hundred seedling Red barks planted in October 1866, although damaged by fire and injured by transplantation, seem to have done very well.

On the Shevaroy Hills.

It was considered that the higher parts of British Burma offered a suitable climate for Cinchona, and it was thought of much importance to interest the Karen population in the cultivation. The matter was therefore taken up with some vigour by the Forest Department. The following account of the experiment in that province has been drawn up by Mr. Ribbentrop, the Officiating Conservator of Forests[1]:—

In British Burma.

"The first mention of Cinchona cultivation in Burma is in the annual forest report of 1865-66, where it is stated that a few Cinchona plants were planted on the top of the Bogalay Hills east of Toungboo. In the report for 1867-68 it is noted that of these plants only two survived, and these trees are still in existence and doing well. In December 1868, 188 plants of *Cinchona succirubra* were planted out at Phunado, at an elevation of 2,100 feet; and of these there were surviving, at the close of March 1870, 87 plants in the upper site and 59 in the lower. A large number of cuttings were obtained from these plants and successfully propagated in new series. Two Karen lads, who had been placed under the care of Mr. McIvor, Ootacamund, in September 1868, returned to Rangoon in November 1869, having gone through a course of training. Unfortunately one of these lads, Fandee, died on the 2nd April 1870. A spot called Thandoungyee had been in the meantime selected as the head-quarters for Cinchona planting, and Phunado was in great part abandoned. Thandoungyee is situated 18 miles north-east of Toungboo, and the hills on which the present plantation is located vary from about 3,700 feet to 4,400 feet above the sea-level. One hundred acres were here made over to the Forest Department in March 1870, but owing to seed having failed to germinate, there was nothing done till 1871. In this year the cuttings raised at Phunado in 1870 were removed to Thandoungyce and planted out, and by the end of the planting season 500 plants had been put out in the main plantation, while the raising of seedlings was being carried on in the propagation-house. It was in the beginning of 1872 that Dr. Adamson received charge of the Sittang Division, involving the charge of the Cinchona plantation, and at that time

---

[1] Letter to the Secretary to the Chief Commissioner, dated 27th November 1875.

INTRODUCTION INTO INDIA.

the establishment consisted of the trained assistant Takai, two other assistants under instruction, and from two to four coolies as required. During 1872 large numbers of seedlings were raised in nursery beds and in the propagation-house, but only a few cuttings were planted out in the main plantation. At the close of the official year 1872-73, there were about 500 young trees in the main plantation, and 18,000 to 20,000 seedlings and cuttings available for planting out in the rains of 1873 and ensuing years. In 1873 an area of about 9 acres was taken in hand, felled, burnt, and planted up, and altogether upwards of 6,000 seedlings and cuttings were put out. In 1874 a fresh clearing of about 27 acres was made in the usual manner, and about 15,000 seedlings and cuttings planted out. In 1875, a still more extensive clearing having been made, 23,000 seedlings and cuttings were transplanted from the nursery beds to the clearing, while about 3,200 were utilised in filling up blanks of the previous two years' cultivation. Such is a short *résumé* of the progress of Cinchona planting in Burma during the last five years, the total number of trees reported alive at the end of October 1875 being about 44,000.

"The following statement shews the proportion of the different varieties of trees planted out in different years:—

	1873.	1874.	1875.
Cinchona *succirubra*	2,024	7,490	18,023
" *calisaya*	198	50	640
" *condaminea*	2,809	4,900	7,806
	5,031	12,440	26,469

"It has been found by experience that the variety *Cinchona succirubra* succeeds best in the Karen Hills. The plants are put out at a distance of 7 by 7, giving 49 square feet per plant. There are thus at least 50 acres covered with Cinchona trees, to which has to be added the area consisting of roads and that covered by the village and other offices. The original area marked off (100 acres) has thus been already fully occupied.

"The soil is a light red soil, the result of decomposition of granitic rock, with, however, a great preponderance of rather coarse quartz sand. The surface soil is only to a very small depth, nowhere exceeding a foot, discoloured either by the decomposition of vegetable matter or by the ashes of burnt-down vegetation. Huge rounded granitic boulders are seen here, as everywhere, in the Karen hills, striking out from the ground or lying loosely on or along the ridges or carried down to the choung.

"The lowest and highest temperatures of the past year were as follow:—

	Fahrenheit.		
	6 A.M.	2 P.M.	6 P.M.
January 14th	43°	73°	55°
April 19th	70°	84°	76°

"The rainy season lasts from May to October.

"I subjoin a statement of the heights and girths of 15 trees of those planted out at Thandoungyee in 1871, taken in November 1872 and again in October 1874:—

No.	NOVEMBER 1872.				OCTOBER 1873.			
	HEIGHT.		GIRTH.		HEIGHT.		GIRTH.	
	Ft.	In.	Ft.	In.	Ft.	In.	Ft.	In.
I	5	0	...	4	13	0	1	0
II	4	7	...	3½	12	4	1	0
III	5	0	...	4	12	0	1	0
IV	4	7	...	4	10	4	0	11
V	5	0	...	4	10	10	1	0
VI	5	0	...	4	11	11	0	11
VII	4	7½	...	4	12	3	1	1
VIII	4	10	...	3½	13	4	1	1
IX	5	1½	...	3½	11	10	1	2
X	5	0	...	4	11	8	1	0
XI	4	9	...	4	12	10	1	2
XII	4	9	...	4	13	1	1	2
XIII	3	11½	...	3½	13	2	1	0
XIV	4	7	...	4	11	5	1	0
XV	5	1	...	3½	13	7	1	1

"On the 31st October 1875 there were in nursery beds 10,000 young seedlings of *Cinchona succirubra* and 4,700 cuttings of *Cinchona condaminea*. About 3,000 seedlings were distributed at the beginning of the rains of 1875 to Karens, who promised to plant them under the auspices of the missionaries (Reverend Father Biffi and Reverend Mr. Bunker), and Mr. Adamson reports that he heard from the Reverend Father Biffi that those he planted were doing well. There can be no doubt that the Cinchona trees at Thandoungyee have succeeded very well as yet. Mr. Kurz, of the Calcutta Botanical Garden, was of opinion that they would do so, but that they would never attain the size of full-grown trees, but always be stunted and branched like the surrounding evergreen vegetation.

"Three specimens of bark were sent in 1873 to the Government Quinologist at Madras, and the following report on them was received:—

"'The specimens were three in number and were respectively labelled, *1st*, bark from upper plantation, Phunado; *2nd*, bark from lower plantation, Phunado; *3rd*, bark from one of the two trees at Bogalay. Of the age or part of the trees producing these specimens I am ignorant, but imagine the age to be about five years. The bark, which was that of *Cinchona succirubra*, had a thin and bad appearance, and gave me the impression of being grown at too low an elevation. Submitted to analysis they yielded the following percentages of alkaloid in 100 parts of quite dry bark:—

	Upper plantation, Phunado.	Lower plantation, Phunado.	One of the two trees at Bogalay.
Total alkaloids	4·29	4·23	3·13
Quinine and Quinicine	0·32	1·18	0·98
Cinchona and Cinchonidine	3·97	3·05	2·15
Pure Quinine Sulphate obtained Crystallised	0·27	0·49	0·56
Pure Cinchonidine Sulphate	1·75	1·05	0·73

"'The barks thus contain a satisfactory amount of alkaloid, but practically yield scarcely any Quinine Sulphate. From this circumstance and their bad appearance, they give little hope of fitness for export. For local employment as a febrifuge they are quite suitable. This opinion is of course based on the assumption that the specimens are fair samples of the barks produced by the trees.'

"I doubt," continues Mr. Ribbentrop, "very much whether an extension of Cinchona plantations in Burma will ever repay the unavoidably large outlay, labour (and that of a very inferior kind) being so costly as compared with other parts of India; moreover, it has been necessary for the last two years to supply the coolies employed at Thandoungyee with their staple food, rice, from Tounghoo, owing to the famine that has, within that period, existed in the Karen country, and which still continues, with no prospect of a speedy termination. This, though not adding to the expense of the plantation, as the coolies repay all expenditure on account of purchase and transport of rice or paddy, has greatly added to the work of the divisional officer, and much difficulty has been experienced in procuring carriage, especially during the rains. Taking this into consideration, but bearing at the same time in mind the wishes of Government to train Karen lads in the planting and raising of Cinchona with a view to introduce the plant amongst the Karens and other hill tribes, I have ordered for the present year an extension of only 3 acres, which will suffice for the training of the lads, perhaps even by more instruction, as Takai will have more of his time to give to their education. At the same time a considerable quantity of seedlings will be reared for gratuitous distribution.

"I annex a memorandum of expenditure during the past four years, which has been wholly on account of Thandoungyee, except Rs. 480 for the pay of one man at Phunado:—

	Rs.
1871-72	1,834
1872-73	2,041
1873-74	2,358
1874-75	5,158"

INTRODUCTION INTO INDIA. 33

In the Khasia Hills.

In 1867 a Cinchona plantation was opened at Nunklow on the north-west slope of the Khasia Hills. This was stocked with 600 plants of *C. succirubra* and 50 of *C. micrantha* from the Sikkim plantation. A supply of seed of *C. officinalis* from the same source was furnished at a later date. The plantation was begun by, and remained under the care of, Mr. A. Biermann (one of the Rungbee staff) for three and a half years. Mr. Biermann put out several patches on the slopes of the Khasias at elevations varying from 4,585 feet above the sea down to the level of the plain of Assam. On the 1st August 1869 there was in the various Khasia plantations a total stock (including trees permanently planted, seedlings and nursery stock plants) of about 27,000 Cinchonas, chiefly Red barks. As the Sikkim plantations were promising so well, it was not considered desirable to extend operations on the Khasias. The European gardener was therefore withdrawn, and the plantations put in charge of a small native establishment sufficient to keep them fairly free from the heavier weeds. Mr. Biermann's opinion was that *succirubra* promised well on these hills at suitable elevations. The trees grew freely as low as 800 feet and as high as 4,800. At levels above 4,800 feet they failed from excessive cold: at lower levels, and especially on the plain of Assam itself, they presented from the first a sickly appearance and rapidly died out, thus confirming the conclusion arrived at in other places that Cinchona will not answer on level ground.

In the North-West Provinces.

Cinchona cultivation received a very patient trial for several years in the North-West Provinces. The experiments were carried out by the staff of the Botanical Garden at Saharunpore, and for some time were under the immediate charge of a gardener who had been for several years employed in the Government Cinchona plantation in Sikkim, and who was therefore familiar with all the practical details of propagation and cultivation as carried on there. Reviewing the various experiments which had been made in these provinces, Dr. Jameson, Superintendent of the Saharunpore Garden, thus writes [1]:—

"For several consecutive years Cinchona cultivation has been carried on in the Dún and Kohistan of the North-West Provinces, or from altitudes of 2,500 feet above the level of the sea up to 6,500 feet, and in all localities it has failed. It has been tried at Chandwallah and other localities in the Dehra Dún at 2,500; at Chejuri in Garhwal at an altitude of 4,500; at Mussooree, altitude 6,500 feet. In the Kumaon Babar, altitude 2,000; at Hawal Bagh in Kumaon at an altitude of 4.500; at Ayar Toli and Raneekhet, altitude 6,000; and at Urkulli, altitude 6,500 to 7,000 feet. In all these localities, barring the Babar of Kumaon, the plants progressed during the hot weather and rains. In the cold weather it was deemed necessary to protect them from the frost, and this was done for three years, and until many of the plants had attained a height of from 4½ to 6 feet. These, with many others, ranging from 2½ to 3 feet, were then left uncovered during the cold weather, and the result was the destruction of every plant in all the localities mentioned. At Ranikhet, plants of the *Cinchona succirubra* species from 4 to 5 feet in height were also cut down, even though partially protected, in a similar manner to those in the Dehra Dún, &c. This, therefore, shews that the plant is not at all fitted for the Dún or Kohistan of the North-West Provinces or Punjab. To rear the plant, particularly the species *Cinchona succirubra* and *Cinchona officinalis*, there is no difficulty, and at the present moment

---

[1] *Memorandum on Cinchona Cultivation in the Dún and Kohistan of the North-West Provinces*, dated 14th August 1873.

there are at Hawal Bagh upwards of 700 plants, under glass, in a thriving condition. But these plants are of no practical use, as during the extensive trials which they have received for several consecutive years all have been destroyed by the frost during the cold season. To continue the growth of the plant as an experiment, in view to the cultivation for economic purposes, would be a mistake, and the time, therefore, has come to close the experiment, which has been carried on with the utmost care, labour, and attention, and to declare that the Dúns and Kohistan of the North-Western Provinces and Punjab are not fittted for the cultivation of Cinchona plants for commercial purposes."

In the Kangra valley. Cinchona received an extended trial on the plantation of Colonel Nassau-Lees in the Kangra Valley. This gentleman threw much spirit into his efforts to introduce the plant. He provided himself from Java, Ceylon, and the Nilgiris with seeds or seedlings of all the leading species, and he imported from Scotland a trained gardener to superintend the cultivation. He was also supplied by Mr. Markham with seeds of *C. Pitayensis*,[1] a species which thrives at high altitudes on the Andes, and which it was hoped would thrive in the comparatively severe winter climate of the Kangra Valley. Colonel Lees' plantation, called New Quitto, is in latitude $30° 7' 8''$ north and at an altitude of 4,500 feet above the sea. Experiments were made by others in the Kangra Valley, and for some time the prospects of success appeard moderately hopeful. Ultimately, however, the majority of the plants succumbed to frost, and the final result is almost identical with that obtained in the North-West Provinces.

In the Mahableshwar Hills. In the Bombay Presidency, the Mahableshwar hills were chosen as the locality most suitable for Cinchona. A site was accordingly selected in 1864 at Lingmulla on the banks of the Yenna stream. This spot is described as having "a northern aspect, protection from the prevailing winds, a good soil and subsoil, and the least possible (for Mahableshwar) rainfall, *viz.*, about 150 inches." At the close of the year 1864 there were 60 young plants, and by February 1866 they had been increased to 270 by layering.

The plants did not thrive well, and in 1874 the Bombay Government asked Mr. McIvor, of the Nilgiri plantation, to visit and report on their condition. At the date of Mr. McIvor's visit there were in permanent plantation at Mahableshwar the following trees [2]:—

Cinchona succirubra	. . .	13,416
„ Condaminea	. .	491
Total	. .	13,907

Mr. McIvor considered that, as regards soil, exposure, and cultivation, the Mahableshwar plants could not have been more favourably situated, but in his opinion the climate is unfavourable, presenting, as it does, such extremes of drought and moisture, and he attributed the prevalence of disease among the trees to this cause. He recommended the immediate abandonment of the plantation. The Government did not, however, at

---

[1] Collected by Mr. Cross.
[2] The above return does not include nursery stock.

once act on his advice, but decided to keep it on for another year in order to try whether a plan proposed by Mr. Woodrow (the Superintendent of the Botanical Garden) would not prove beneficial. Mr. Woodrow thought that a form of canker was the cause of the unhealthiness of the trees, and that by protecting the soil from sun and rain by a covering of dead fern fronds, the roots of the trees could be defended from the extremes of heat and cold and of moisture and draught, and that thus an improvement might be effected. A year's trial of this plan shewed no good results, and the plantation, on which about Rs. 64,000 had been spent, was finally abandoned.

In Ceylon.
In Ceylon the cultivation of Cinchona was begun in 1861, and so long ago as 1864, Dr. Thwaites, F.R.S., the distinguished Director of the Botanical Gardens at Peradenia and Hakgalla, was able to report that the "plants exhibited the most perfect health and vigour." "The site of the plantation at Hakgalla," writes Mr. Markham (who visited it in 1865) "has been so admirably selected, and resembles so closely the native habitat of the Cinchona in South America, that the healthy growth of the plants there must have been a certainty from the first." The growth of the two species *succirubra* and *officinalis* at Hakgalla has been excellent, and the ground under the trees by the sides of the roads in the plantation and all waste spots near it are crowded with spontaneous cinchona seedlings—a circumstance which clearly proves the thorough suitability of the spot to the requirements of cinchona. From this Hakgalla plantation hundreds of thousands of seedlings and many ounces of seed have with the greatest liberality been given away to planters in the colony, by whom cinchona cultivation has been taken up as an adjunct to coffee-planting. The recent progress has (as will be seen from the following extract from the Ceylon Directory for 1875) been most striking:—

"The Director of the Royal Botanical Garden in his report for 1873 mentioned that he had applications during that year for over a million of cinchona plants, 800,000 of which he was able to supply. Previously, it is estimated, half a million of plants were issued. During 1874 the Director reports that 826,000 additional have been issued, and, counting the number of plants obtained from private nurseries and estates, very nearly three millions will thus be made up."

I am informed by Mr. Fergusson, the Editor of the *Ceylon Observer*, and himself a successful Cinchona planter, that during 1875 about a million and a half plants, raised in Government and private nurseries, were planted out, and that the acreage under Cinchona from 1872 to 1875 may be stated as follows :—

        1872 . . . . . . 500 acres.
        1873 . . . . . 1,500 „
        1874 . . . . . 2,000 „
        1875 . . . . 3,000 „

Large extensions are now being carried on, and by the end of 1876 the same authority estimates that the Cinchona trees in Ceylon will number nearly six millions. The Red bark tree, from its rapid growth and the prospect it gave of yielding a quick return on capital, was at first the favourite with planters. But now that the merits of the Pale barks are becoming better understood, *C. officinalis* is also being largely planted. *C. Calisaya* has as yet made little way in Ceylon. Ceylon-grown bark has been repeatedly analysed and shewn to be rich in alkaloids. No attempt has been made, nor probably will any be made, to extract the alkaloids locally; repeated consignments of bark have, however, been sent to England for sale and have brought good prices.[1]

In other colonies. The cultivation of Cinchona has been begun in Jamaica, and in others of the West Indian British colonies, in the French colonies, Bourbon and Réunion, in St. Helena, the Mauritius, and elsewhere. In all these localities, *succirubra* is the species grown; it is therefore probable that the European market will soon be flooded with supplies of Red bark, and it is not unlikely that the price of that sort will fall correspondingly.

---

[1] See Appendix G.

CHAPTER IV.

THE CULTIVATION OF THE CINCHONA TREE.

Climate suitable for Cinchona cultivation.

WITH regard to the climate suitable for Cinchonas, it may be laid down as a universal rule that none of the medicinal species will stand frost. They prefer rather a cool climate in which the contrast between summer and winter, and between day and night temperatures, is not very great. These conditions are in some measure obtained in the Nilgiris and in Sikkim. At Ootacamund, about 7,500 feet above the sea, the minimum lowest temperature in the shade, calculated on an average of the three years, is about 49° and the maximum 69° Fahr.; and at Neddiwattum, situated about 2,000 feet lower, the minimum, calculated also over three years, is found to be about 54° Fahr. and the maximum 66° Fahr. Full details will be found in the Appendix.[1] Observations taken in 1866 and 1867 at an elevation of 3,332 feet in the Rungbee Valley, in Sikkim, shew a minimum temperature of 40° and 41° Fahr., and a maximum of 88° Fahr., the mean minima for the two years being 59·20° and 57·53°, the mean maxima 71·7° and 72·28° Fahr., and the mean temperatures 65·6° and 64·89° respectively. Detailed statements of observations for these years, made at five stations in the Rungbee reserve, at different altitudes, are given in an Appendix.[2] The latter figures give an idea of a climate fairly suitable for *succirubra*, but rather cold for *Calisaya*. A more congenial climate for both species is indicated by the figures obtained at a lower station (elevation above the sea 2,556 feet) which, for the years 1866 and 1867, are as follow:—

Temperature.

Minimum temperature	40° and 41° Fahr.
Maximum „	92·3° and 94° „
Mean minimum temperature	59·3° and 60·94° „
„ maximum „	80·6° and 81·59° „
„ temperature	70·1° and 71·26° „

In various parts of Ceylon a favourable climate for Cinchona is obtained, as will be seen from the following extract from a most reliable local publication[3]:—

"In the Dimbula district, for example, there is a mean temperature of 65·8° Fahr., with nothing colder in the shade in winter than 44·5° (12° above freezing point), and nothing hotter in the shade in summer than 89°, both extremes being exceptional, and the latter helping to produce a maximum temperature favourable to coffee cultivation, equally so to tea and cinchona without being injurious to human health. Dismissing the rarely occurring extremes, we get a mean maximum in the shade of 73·2° Fahr. against a mean minimum of 58·4° Fahr., resulting, as we have already noticed,

---

[1] See Appendix H.
[2] See Appendix I.
[3] See a pamphlet on the climate of Dimbula published at the *Ceylon Observer* Office, Colombo, 1875.

in a mean shade temperature of 65·8° Fahr. But . . . on a clear January morning, before the sun has dawned, the exposed thermometer may indicate a cold of 33° Fahr. or only one degree above freezing point; while at noon-day in April (our hottest month) the mercury may, under the full influence of the sun's rays, rise to 136° Fahr. But these, again, are the extremes on the grass and in the sun, the mean maximum of the exposed thermometer being only 103·5° Fahr. against a mean minimum of 54·1° Fahr."

Rainfall.

In the matter of moisture, the peculiarities of the Cinchonas were at first rather misunderstood, their preference for incessant rain and mist having been exaggerated. It is found, especially on the Nilgiris, that all the species, and particularly the Red barks, withstand long droughts. All the species assume a yellowish tint during the rains (indicating an excessive supply of moisture), and (in the Nilgiris) all make their most vigorous growth during the seasons in which sunshine and showers alternate. After a continuance of dull steamy days all the species seem to become tender, and a sudden change to bright sunny weather affects the plants in a most marked way, causing their leaves to flag. In Sikkim, *succirubra* makes its most vigorous growth during the latter half of the rains, but both on the Nilgiris and Himalayas the trees continue to grow for two months after the rains cease.

Observations which have been made shew that (calculated on the returns of five years) there are at Ootacamund no fewer than 218 dry days in the year, and at Neddiwattum about 240 dry days. The rainfall of the former locality (on an average of three years) is about 44 inches per annum, and that of Neddiwattum 105 inches. The amount of moisture in the air is indicated by the returns for the year 1868-69, which are given as an Appendix[1] to this report. The rainfall in Sikkim is much heavier than on the Nilgiris, but is much affected by locality. At Rungbee, altitude 5,000 feet, during 1872, 165·55 inches of rain were registered; while at Rishap, 3,000 feet lower and four miles distant, only 120·6 inches fell.[2] The general features of the climate have been thus described in one of my reports:—

"The climate of the Rungbee Valley is peculiar. Being so completely shut in upon all sides, it is protected in a striking degree from wind, and up to the higher limits of the Cinchona belt, the air is rarely stirred by even the gentlest breeze—a state of things in striking contrast to that obtaining in the Nilgiris, where in exposed places great and permanent injury is done to the Cinchona plants by the high winds. At the lower levels frost is completely unknown, and the climate is indeed sub-tropical, while on the higher southern and western slopes frost, and even snow, are the order of the day during the cold season. Occasionally heavy hail-storms pass over the valley, tearing to pieces the thin broad leaves of the Red bark trees. The mischief thus done is, however, rapidly recovered from. The rainfall is heavy, but not equally so in all parts of the valley. The warm vapour-laden air passing up from the plains has its moisture condensed into clouds by the cool, high, forest-clad ridges that form the northern and western boundary of the valley, and for a great part of the year the higher part of these are enveloped in drizzling fog. Even at the driest season one is struck by the amount of mist which, condensed at the higher elevations, almost every evening creeps well down their slopes, while the whole of the opposite side and of the lower part of the valley continue quite clear. During the monsoon the rainfall on these high southern ridges must be very great. Some idea of its extent may be formed from the fact that at a bungalow standing in the south-western corner of the valley, at

---

[1] See Appendix H.   [2] See Appendix J.

THE CULTIVATION OF THE CINCHONA TREE. 39

an elevation of only 5,000 feet, and thus far below the crest, the rainfall for the year averages about 200 inches. At lower levels in the valley the rainfall is very much less, and no part of the Government Cinchona cultivation is exposed to such a downpour. For example, at the Rishap plantation but (2,000 feet above the sea), where a rain-gauge has been kept for some years, the average is shewn to be about 120 inches, and as the mouth of the valley and the Teesta are approached, the climate becomes very much drier. The northern side of the valley, being itself comparatively low and cleared of forest, and being besides beyond the influence of the high ranges, shares in the drier climate."

Cinchona appears to find a congenial home in the uniformly moist climate of Ceylon in the districts of Dikoya and Maskeliya; for example, the rainfall ranges, as far as the figures available enable us to judge, from 120 to 145 inches for Dikoya, and from 130 to 150 inches from Maskeliya. This rainfall is well distributed over the year.

In the adjoining district of Dimbula the annual rainfall is about 108 inches, and the number of dry days in the year about 145. In all three the rain falls uniformly and gently, violent storms being rare. The meteorological returns in the Appendix[1] (for which I am indebted to Mr. Fergusson, Editor of the *Ceylon Observer*) will give a good idea of the climate.

Wind and hail. The Nilgiri and many of the Ceylon plantations are much exposed to continuous and high winds; those of Sikkim are, on the other hand, but rarely subjected to even a moderate breeze. Wind, when excessive and frequent, appears to do considerable and permanent damage, especially to *succirubra*, the leaves of which are large and tender. Hail, if heavy, strips a plantation of its leaves, but the check to growth caused by this is but temporary, as new leaves speedily appear. In standing the violence of storms, says Mr. McIvor, "the Crown barks rank first, the Red second, the Grey third, and the Yellow fourth."

Elevation above the sea. As regards elevation above the sea, it is found that, in the Nilgiris, *succirubra* succeeds best at altitudes of from 4,500 to 6,000 feet. An elevation of 7,000 feet is found to be too high, the growth being too slow to be profitable. Pale or Crown barks thrive in a zone above this, and seem to succeed well even up to 8,500 feet. *Calisaya* on the Nilgiris has not been a success at any elevation, but it does rather better, as also do the Grey barks, within the *succirubra* zone than at higher elevations. In Sikkim, 16° further north, experience has shewn that *succirubra* and the Grey barks thrive well from 1,500 to 3,500 feet, and can be got to grow both as low as 800 feet and as high as 5,000 feet; *Calisaya* thrives between 1,500 and 3,000 feet; *Officinalis* does not thrive at any elevation.

Soil and drainage. All the species are most impatient of stagnant moisture at their roots, and therefore require an open subsoil, a sloping exposure, and the other conditions of perfect drainage. They cannot be got to grow on flat land. Like most other plants, they prefer a rich soil, and for this reason they do better in newly-cleared forest than in grass lands of the sort so extensive in the Nilgiris. The Crown or Pale barks, however, are more tolerant than the others of a soil poor in vegetable humus, and grow fairly well on grass-land as well

---

[1] See Appendix K.

as on "laterite soils." The freer and more friable the surface soil the better, but an open well-drained subsoil is above all things indispensable to their successful growth. As soon as the roots of a Cinchona tree get down into subsoil in which there is any tendency for moisture to collect, the plant most certainly begins to sicken and die. The basis of the soil of the Nilgiris is decomposed gneiss; in Sikkim it is composed both of gneiss and of decaying mica schist.

In Sikkim and also in the Nilgiris and elsewhere in India where Cinchona has been introduced, the plants are subject to two forms of disease. Both diseases were common on the older parts of the Sikkim plantations, and attracted some attention during the meeting of the Cinchona Commission there in 1871. Mr. McIvor apparently considers them more serious than they have turned out to be. They are thus described in my report on the Sikkim plantation for 1871-72:—

Disease.

"After very careful examination it appears plain to me that two distinct forms of disease occur in the Sikkim plantations,—the one, a constitutional malady, affecting the whole plant and usually fatal; the other, local and by no means fatal. The former disease is confined entirely to trees which have been originally planted in damp situations, or in situations which have become damp subsequently by the oozing of drainage water. Disease first attacks the roots of such trees. Its existence becomes apparent by the discoloration of their leaves, which ultimately all fall off. Gradual shrivelling of the cortical and woody tissues then takes place from the root upwards, and before this process has gone far the death of the plant has begun. This disease is in fact apparently nearly identical with that known to gardeners in England as 'canker;' it is not in any way infectious or contagious, as some appear to think. It depends entirely on a local cause—namely, excess of moisture in the soil; and where that does not exist, it cannot occur. In the Cinchona planted on the western end of the Rungbee valley, patches of trees killed by this disease are not uncommon. Such patches are invariably co-extensive with damp, watery soil.

"The second form of disease does not affect the entire constitution of the plant, but manifests itself in patches on the stem and branches. The appearance of one of these patches is as if some escharotic had been dropped on the bark, which is of a dark, unnatural colour, shrivelled, dry, and brittle; occasionally these appearances extend to the wood, but as a rule they do not. In size the patches vary; many are about the size of a shilling, others are much larger. They are not numerous on one tree, and are often confined to a single branch. When small, no apparent affection of the general health of the plant occurs, and growth goes on unchecked. Where, however, a large patch occurs on a small tree, involving the bark pretty nearly all round the stem, death results. Death from this disease is, however, as far as my observations go, not common; and it is a well-established fact that a tree which has been extensively affected will often, when cut down, throw up from its stump perfectly healthy shoots; while in hundreds of trees at Rungbee I have seen illustrations of recovery, the little patches of diseased bark being thrown off and replaced by perfectly healthy tissue, and the plant apparently as robust as if it never had been attacked. I had not sufficient leisure last year during the season at which this affection is most prevalent—namely, the rains—to make successive observations on the state of the diseased tissues, and I am prepared with no theories about its cause; I hope, however, to find out something during the approaching rains. This disease is not confined like the last to certain localities, but is found on plants in all parts of the plantation. I do not think it is to be feared much, and I certainly do not concur in Mr. McIvor's views concerning its dangerous nature. In my opinion it must be accepted as one of the drawbacks attending the Cinchona experiment."

It is quite possible that, as some observers are inclined to think, both these diseases may be essentially one in nature, the second being a mild form of the first and caused by some of the roots getting into uncongenial sour soil and so becoming diseased. On this view recovery would

THE CULTIVATION OF THE CINCHONA TREE.

be accounted for by the gradual penetration of the roots into more suitable soil.

Mode of collecting seed. Cinchona seeds ripen during the dry season that follows the rains.[1] They should be carefully gathered just as the seed vessels begin spontaneously to burst. After being gathered the latter should be laid out in shallow boxes to dry until the seeds fall out of their own accord. Exposure to strong sunlight is unnecessary, and the seeds probably dry best if laid during the day in a place exposed to a current of air. At night they should be put under shelter for protection from rain and dew. The seeds of all the species are oblong, flattened, and very light. Mr. McIvor calculates that "an ounce of clean seeds produces on an average from 20,000 to 25,000 plants." These seeds do not retain their vitality long, and should be sown as soon as possible after collection. For transport to a distance they travel best if packed in porous cloth and sent by post. Waxcloth makes a bad covering, as it prevents ventilation.

Sowing seed. "Cinchona seeds," says Mr. McIvor, "germinate best at a temperature varying from 65° to 70° Fahr.; they will also germinate, though slowly, at a temperature of 55° Fahr., and will sustain a temperature of 80° Fahr." During the cold season, seeds should therefore be sown under glass, but during the hot weather and rains they should be sown in open beds which are sheltered merely by thatched roofs. In either case the seeds must be sown in fine, rich, thoroughly-decayed vegetable mould, either pure or mixed with an equal volume of clean sharp sand which does not feel clayey or sticky when a little of it is taken up and compressed between the fingers. Mould can usually be easily collected in the forest, and is specially abundant at the base of old clumps of bamboo. After being sifted, the soil so collected should then be spread in layers about two or three inches in depth and five feet wide, on beds of ground which have been previously well cleared. These beds may be of any length that is convenient. They should run east and west, and should have their open side directed towards the north. They should slope to one side, so that no water whatever may lodge in them at any season, and should be protected from rain and sunshine and from all drip by a single sloping thatch,[2] the slope of which should be in the same direction as, though of course much greater than, the slope of the bed. It is convenient to have a path in front of each bed. The drainage of each bed should be distinct from that of its neighbour. In most places where Cinchona is likely to be grown, perfect drainage can always be secured by making the beds on terraces on a hill-side. Before sowing the seeds, the soil of the seed-bed should be brought to a uniform degree of firmness by working it through and gently pressing it down with the expanded fingers. If this be not attended to, but on the contrary the soil be left loose in one part and compressed in another, water will penetrate

---

[1] In Sikkim, *succirubra* seed begins to ripen about the end of the rainy season; *Calisaya* seed does not ripen until about January.

[2] It is not convenient to have the thatch too low. If it be made five feet above the soil at the front or higher and two feet at the back or lower side, coolies can easily work under it, and plenty of light and air are besides admitted. During the rains it is especially necessary to admit a free current of air.

unequally, and unevenness of surface will ultimately result. The surface should from the first be smooth and even, but not hard and compressed. The seed should then be scattered pretty thickly on its surface, and afterwards a very little fine earth or sand may be sprinkled above it.[1] It is not desired to cover the seeds, but merely to steady them by a little earth above them here and there, and to get them into proper contact with the soil. It is a very good plan after sowing the seed to press the surface of the bed very gently with the expanded palms or with a smooth board. Water should be given in the early part of the day rather than in the evening. Watering must be done judiciously, and anything like deluging must be carefully avoided; at the same time a uniform state of moisture should be maintained. This is best managed by using a very finely bored garden syringe and forcing the stream of water through it at some distance from the bed to be operated on, so that the moisture may fall on the soil in the form of fine spray. Very cold water should be avoided; it may therefore often be necessary to allow water to stand for some time in a warm sunny place before using it, so as to bring it as near to the temperature of the air as possible. The seeds will germinate in from two to six weeks, according to temperature. Besides the morning watering, it may be necessary to water the seedlings slightly once or even twice during the day, but watering late in the evening should be avoided. From the time the seed is sown, it will sometimes be necessary to give the beds a more complete protection from wind, rain, or sunshine than is afforded by the thatch above described. When this is necessary, it can be easily done by putting up mats at the exposed parts of the bed. If seeds are sown under glass, they should be well shaded, and especial care should be taken in watering seedlings under glass to allow the leaves to become quite dry before shutting the frames. Young seedlings are especially liable to damp off, and every precaution should be taken to prevent this accident. In Sikkim, more particularly in very damp weather, the seed-beds are occasionally infested by the mycelium of a fungus, the minute threads of which ramify in the soil and kill many of the tender seedlings. Gentle stirring of the soil is found to be of some use in checking the ravages of this pest.

Treatment of seed-beds and seedlings.

The next operation is to prick the young seedlings out into nursery beds. This first transplantation should be done when the plants have got two, or even three, pairs of leaves. The best way to remove them is to insert a small flat-

Pricking out.

---

[1] In his notes on the propagation of Cinchonas (Gantz Brothers, Madras, 1867) Mr. McIvor recommends that, if the seeds be fresh, they should be steeped in cold water for twelve hours before being sown, but if the seeds have come from a great distance, or have been kept for some time, six hours steeping will, he considers, be sufficient. "The most convenient way," writes Mr. McIvor, "to steep the seeds is to place them loosely in a bag and immerse the same in water. When the seeds have been soaked the prescribed time, take the bag out and drain off the water; the seeds will be found to have swollen considerably, and in order to separate them, mix them with about twice their bulk of dry sand. In this way the moisture around the seeds is absorbed, and on being stirred gently the seeds separate from each other freely and intermix with the sand. In this condition they are sown on the surface of the soil, and lightly covered over with a mere sprinkling of dry sand."

THE CULTIVATION OF THE CINCHONA TREE. 43

pointed stick into the soil under the plants and then to press the point of the stick gently upwards, so stirring and loosening the soil as to allow the plants to be easily removed from it without breaking their tender rootlets. It is a good plan to begin this operation at one end or side of a seed-bed and to work across it in one direction until all the plants with two or three pairs of leaves are taken out. Probably a few days later some seeds hitherto dormant will have germinated; these can then be removed in their turn. The seedlings taken out should be transplanted into nursery beds formed in every respect like the seed-beds, but with a thicker layer of vegetable soil. They should be pricked out in lines at distances of a little less than $1\frac{1}{2}$ inches, with a space between the lines of about 2 inches. A bed, 5 feet wide, will thus give transverse lines holding about 50 plants each. The holes for the roots of the seedlings are readily made with a blunt-pointed stick. In this, as in subsequent transplantations, care should be taken not to double up the roots, but to make the holes deep enough to receive them stretched out to their full length. The roots of the seedling being put into the hole, the earth should be filled in, and care should be taken to press down the earth and so fill the hole thoroughly to the very bottom. A careless planter will often press the soil firmly into the upper part of the hole, leaving the bottom of the latter imperfectly filled with soil. It is often of advantage to prick the seedlings out into shallow boxes instead of the open ground. They are thus under command and can be put under glass frames, if necessary, to establish them. After having been pricked out, the plants should remain untouched until they are about 4 inches high, when a second transplantation will be necessary. On this second occasion they should be planted out in the same manner as before, only at distances of about 4 by 4 inches each way. When from 9 to 12 inches in height, the seedlings are ready for transplanting into the situations they are permanently to occupy. If left too long in nursery beds, they are liable to become unhealthy. On the other hand, it is a mistake to put out too small plants. To harden them for the final transplantation, the thatch by which the seedlings have hitherto been protected should be removed, and they should be exposed freely to the weather for at least a fortnight prior to removal, but dull cloudy weather must be chosen (for the beginning at least of this hardening process), for sudden exposure to a bright sun would be disastrous. From the sowing of the seed until this final transplantation, probably eight to twelve months must elapse, and during this time judicious watering is necessary whenever the soil is dry,—care, however, being taken not to overdo it.

Propagation by cuttings. *Cinchona succirubra* is propagated from cuttings with great readiness, and this method is probably easier and, to the unexperienced cultivator, safer than propagation by seedlings. The best wood to choose for cuttings is the thin, but not too succulent, wood of the current year's growth, that yielded by young shoots springing from the lower part of the stem being preferable to the branches of the tree. The cuttings should be cut just below the joint, or point where a pair of leaves (Cinchona leaves always are in pairs) originates. The larger leaves should be removed all except their bases, but the younger unexpanded leaves, if any, should be allowed to remain. Cuttings of this species answer very well if put out in thatched beds of the sort already described for seedlings. They may be also tried in shallow boxes about two inches deep, filled with a layer of fine vegetable mould mixed with sand. A layer of pure sand above the mould is of great use, as it promotes drainage, and cuttings are very apt to rot off at the level of the soil if it is not thoroughly drained. Red bark cuttings form roots in from two to four months, according to season and temperature. For out-door cuttings, the months from April to August are found in Sikkim to be the most favourable. In drier localities, April will probably be found too early; but the most suitable season must be determined for every locality by experience.

In his admirable treatise on the principles and practices of horticulture,[1] a book deserving of careful study by all interested in the growing of plants, Dr. Lindley makes the following remarks, which are particularly appropriate to the artificial propagation of *Cinchona Calisaya*: "It is known," says Dr. Lindley, "that plants possess some quality analogous to animal irritability, to which, for want of a better, the name of excitability has been given. In proportion to the amount of excitability in a given plant is the power which its cuttings possess of striking. The great promoter of vegetable excitability is heat. Therefore the more heat a given plant has been exposed to, within certain limits, the more readily its cuttings strike root. This explains what seems to have puzzled Mr. Newman.[2] 'The young wood,' he says, 'of trees growing in the open air will not do for cuttings: and yet if those same trees are forced in a hot-house, their cuttings are almost sure to succeed.'" This is the case with *Cinchona Calisya*, in Sikkim at least. When, therefore, it is necessary to resort to artificial methods (as is the case with *Calisaya*) of propagation, the first step is to establish stock plants from which to take cuttings. This is easily done by making layers in the usual way. The operation of layering consists in bending the branch of a tree into the soil and half cutting it through at the bend, the object being to cause the upper part of the branch thus partially separated to form roots on the cut surface. The cut part is then put into the soil and, if necessary, pegged down, a quantity of sand being put round the wound so as to ensure good drainage. It is often found useful to bend the shoot well back before putting the wound in the ground, so as in a measure to obstruct the channels by which the sap passes, and thus, by impeding the return of sap from the layer into the main stem, to secure it for the layer itself. As the wood of *Calisaya* is rather brittle, bending, if practised at all, must be done carefully. If the branches of a Cinchona tree, as is usually the case, cannot be conveniently bent down to the natural soil, soil must be elevated to them. This is easily done by filling boxes with well-selected earth and raising them on posts. In the course of three or four months *Calisaya* layers are found to root. While rooting they must be carefully watered: the beginning of the rainy season is therefore the best suited for layering. When well rooted, the layers should be transplanted into glazed frames (made like ordinary cucumber frames), and planted in

Propagation by cuttings from stock plants.

---

[1] *The Theory and Practice of Horticulture*, by John Lindley, F.R.S., &c., &c. Longmans & Co., London, 1875.
[2] The author of an excellent treatise on the propagation of plants.

good soil at distances of about six inches apart. These are called *stock plants*, and about every month, or every second month, according to circumstances, they will yield a crop of cuttings. Each of the cuttings so yielded will of course consist of soft young wood. In taking the cuttings from the stock plants entire shoots should not be removed, but a bud or two should always be left on the part of the shoot remaining on the stock plant to provide new shoots. The cuttings themselves should be about three to four inches long. The fully-developed leaves on the cuttings should be cut so as to leave only their lower halves on the cuttings, but all young leaves should be allowed to remain entire. The cuttings should be put into shallow boxes of the sort already described. The soil in these boxes should consist of fine, perfectly-decayed, vegetable mould, mixed with from one-half to one-third its volume of sand, and on the top of the soil should be spread a layer, about two-thirds of an inch deep, of pure sand to promote drainage. It is preferable to put the cuttings into boxes, as described, than to put them into open soil under frames; for when the cuttings are rooted, the boxes can be removed, so as to harden the cuttings gradually without disturbing their delicate roots.

" What is demanded," says Dr. Lindley in the work[1] already quoted, " when cuttings of plants are to be struck, is a due adjustment of heat, light, and moisture. The first stimulates the vital processes, the second causes the formation of matter out of which roots and leaves are organised, the third is at once the vehicle for the food required by the cutting and a part of it. The difficulty is to know how to adjust these agents. If the heat is too high, organs are formed faster than they can be solidified ; if too low, decay comes on before the reproductive forces can be put in action. When light is too powerful, the fluid contents of the cutting are lost faster than they can be supplied ; when too feeble, there is not a sufficiently quick formation of organisable matter to construct the new roots and leaves with. If water is deficient, the cutting is starved ; if overabundant, it rots." Bearing these principles in mind, therefore, care should be taken to provide mats to lay on the glazed frames, so as to shade them when the sun's rays are too powerful ; an equable moist atmosphere should be kept up inside the frame; ventilation should be provided for by opening the frames for half an hour or an hour early in the morning, and by keeping them at other times slightly ajar by means of a stone or stick ; and, above all, watering should be carefully done by means of a finely-drilled syringe. Deluging should always be avoided, and the leaves should never be allowed to be wet in the evening or at night. Good cuttings will root during warm weather in from three to four weeks ; in the cold season, however, sometimes as long as four or five months elapse before good roots are formed. Propagation in frames or houses furnished with bottom heat need not be described here, as, in a favourable climate for Cinchona cultivation, cuttings can be made to root as above described. When thoroughly rooted, the cuttings should be transplanted into thatched beds, like seedlings at their second transplantation. Their further treatment should be precisely that of seedlings.

---

[1] *Theory and Practice of Horticulture*, page 289.

Propagation by buds. Propagation by buds was practised both on the Nilgiris and Sikkim in the early days of the Cinchona enterprise. It is now no longer necessary to resort to this method.

Preparing ground for permanent plantation. In preparing ground for permanent plantation, the first thing is, of course, to select the place; this should be done with due care and after full consideration has been given to the points imperfectly discussed above. The selected spot must then be cleared of its natural vegetation.[1] The best time for beginning to do this is obviously when the dry season has sufficiently advanced to make a second growth of grass improbable. When the felled forest, whether grass or timber, is sufficiently dry, it may be fired. Stumps and logs remaining unburnt after the fire may be rolled into spots unsuitable for planting, or heaped together and burnt. A better way is to lay them between the lines of plants, and allow them to rot, and thus to profit by the humus formed by their decay. The large fibrous roots of tall grasses and other weeds likely to overpower the young trees about to be planted, should be dug out and killed either by exposure or burning.

Lining out.

The land being thus cleared, any necessary roads may be lined off and made. The sites in which the plants are to be put must then be marked off. This may conveniently be done by means of a cord, about 100 feet long, on which marks are tied at the intervals at which it is wished to plant the trees. This cord is stretched on the ground, and opposite each of the marks on it a piece of split bamboo is struck into the soil. The cord is then moved, another line is staked off at a proper distance from the last, and so on. Coolies follow, whose duty it is to dig pits, about a foot to fifteen inches in depth and eighteen inches wide, of which the stakes already put in should be the centres. The earth (freed from roots and stones) which has been taken out of each hole should be returned to it, so as to form a free mass in which the roots of the plant about to be placed can freely work. A coolie in Sikkim makes from 100 to 130 of such pits per day, according to the nature of the ground. Plants hardened as described are then brought from the nursery lines in shallow boxes, care being taken to bring some earth with their roots and not to expose them to the air longer than is absolutely necessary. The nursery beds should be well deluged with water the night before the plants are removed, so that the soil may adhere to their roots. A set of coolies should be told off to plant these in the pits just mentioned. This is readily done by scraping a hole with the hands, or with a native trowel. The usual precautions should be taken to make this hole deep enough to receive the roots of the plant without doubling, and to press the soil well down as it is thrown in to cover the roots. One man can easily supply two planters with plants; he should walk between two rows of holes and hand to each planter (from a box carried in front of himself) a plant as he requires it. If the plants be taken out of the box in which they have been brought from the nursery, and laid on the ground beside the holes to be planted as the planters work

Digging pits.

Planting.

---

[1] In windy, exposed places, belts of forest may be left on the ridges to give shelter.

up to them (a cheaper plan than that above recommended), the balls of earth round their roots are almost sure to be broken. Planting is too important an operation to be done badly; it is not wise to try to economise on it, and it is probably always unadvisable to do it by contract. A good planter should be able to put in from five hundred to a thousand plants per day, according to the nature of the ground. Nothing need be said of deep hoeing or trenching the soil preparatory to planting, as these operations are too costly for Cinchona, and, besides, are inadmissible in steep ground on account of the wash that follows excessive loosening of the soil. In the earlier days of the Nilgiri plantations the soil was trenched prior to being planted. In his little book on Cinchona cultivation, already quoted, Mr. McIvor recommends trenching, or, where that is considered too expensive, the digging of pits for the plants, each pit to be two feet square and two feet deep. Planting should be done when the soil is moist and when the weather is cloudy or even wet, but heavy rain is not favourable.

In the early Nilgiri planting, the trees were put out at distances of twelve feet apart, subsequently at distances of eight feet, and latterly at six by six feet. In Sikkim, the earlier planting stands six by six feet, but for the past four years a distance of four by four feet has been adopted. The Red bark, even in South America, is never a large tree; *Cinchona officinalis* is but a big shrub; and it is doubtful whether, in India, *Calisaya* will ever attain any very great size. Wide planting is therefore obviously an error. All the Cinchonas, moreover, have the habit of throwing out a quantity of superficial rootlets, and young Cinchona plantations do not thrive until the soil between the trees is sufficiently protected from the sun to allow these superficial rootlets to perform their functions freely. The growth of weeds, as has just been stated, is also checked by shade. By close planting, therefore, two desirable objects are speedily obtained, and, moreover, the trees are encouraged to produce straight clean stems.[1] As the trees begin to press on each other they can be thinned out, and a quantity of bark may thus be got at a comparatively early period with positive advantage to the plants that are allowed to remain on the ground. It is true that the initial cost of close planting is greater than of sparse planting : on the other hand, the cost of keeping clean, especially during the first three years, is less.

Planting distance.

In Sikkim, no shading or protection is necessary for newly-planted Cinchonas. In other localities, protection from the sun may, however, be required. This can readily be afforded by erecting on the sunny side of each plant a rough frame-work of bamboo on which grass or ferns can be tied, by sticking leafy branches into the ground, and so on. The best and cheapest mode for any particular locality must of course be dependent on local conditions.

Shading.

In windy localities it may be necessary, when the plants attain the height of a few feet, to give them support by stakes. The great danger to be avoided in staked plants is the chafing caused by the swaying of the plant. Means must

Staking.

---

[1] On this well-known habit is founded the practice of close planting in forest plantations in Europe, the object being to produce long, straight, unbranching stems from which to cut timber of long scantling.

therefore be taken to prevent this by using a soft material for tying and so forth. A mode of support, suggested by Mr. McIvor, is to run rows of stakes between the rows of trees, and along the stakes to tie a continuous grass rope at a sufficient height from the ground to be clear of the stems and on a level with the leafy heads of the trees. The trees stand in this way free from the rope, but receive support from it when they are much bent by the wind. Staking in any form is expensive, and it is a question whether it is worth while to plant Cinchonas in situations where it is likely to be necessary.

Tillage. As soon as the weeds in the newly-planted land threaten to choke the young plants, they must be cut and a similar cleaning must be repeated whenever necessary. No special rule can be laid down as to the number of cleanings to be given in a season, but for the first three years it is probable that two or three will be necessary, after which once a year will be enough; and finally weeding will not be wanted at all. If laid in lines between the rows of plants, the cut weeds rot and form manure. It is hopeless to think of entirely freeing the ground from weeds and of keeping a Cinchona plantation as clean as a flower garden, and it is quite unnecessary to do so. Myriads of annuals, notably the White Weed (*Ageratum*), grasses, sedges, &c., spring up, but, if kept under by cutting, these do but little harm. All large perennial grasses and other deep-rooting weeds which have survived the first cleaning of the ground, should be taken out as soon as they shew signs of growth. Some of the species of grass resembling the Couch Grass of England are especially noxious, and where they remain in the ground, Cinchona will not grow. In cutting weeds of any kind, the coolies ought to be taught to cut quite close to the ground. Where the majority of the weeds are annuals and the soil is soft and friable, it may be advisable occasionally to substitute hand-weeding for cutting. The disturbance of the surface of the soil caused in pulling the weeds up by the roots, affords a rough kind of cultivation which is advantageous: moreover, the superficial roots of the Cinchonas are less damaged than by hoeing. It need scarcely be stated that, in proportion as the Cinchona trees grow and their leafy heads cover the ground, the undergrowth of weeds becomes less luxuriant. A slight superficial hoeing of the soil immediately round the plants should, however, be given once a year, if possible. The space thus cleared need not exceed one and a half to two feet in diameter, having the tree stem as its centre. To young plants especially, this is very beneficial, and it is found that even the oldest trees in the Sikkim plantation are much benefited by the operation. The first year after planting, a general digging or hoeing should be given during the cold season to eradicate the weeds that may have escaped the first cleaning; during the second year only a light hoeing will be necessary. In all cultural operations it ought to be borne in mind that the roots of Cinchonas are comparatively superficial, and that any very deep hoeing is therefore more likely to do harm than good.

Pruning. Like many other trees, Cinchonas, especially when close-planted, have a strong tendency to throw off their lower branches as they increase in height. Artificial removal of such branches as would in time naturally drop off may be resorted to in places where the young trees stand so close that the circulation of air is seriously impeded. When it becomes necessary to thin a plantation, double stems may be reduced to one, and any large branches that may project so as to injure a neighbouring tree may be cut away, but any extensive pruning of the trees that are to be allowed to stand is to be avoided. It should not be forgotten that the leaves are the chief means by which a tree grows, and that an increased yield of bark is not likely to follow a too free removal of these.

Manuring. The Nilgiri trials of manure went to shew that its application does not stimulate the growth of Cinchona trees. The limited Sikkim experience, on the contrary, indicates that Cinchona, like most other plants, is benefited by manure. It would, however, be premature to form as yet any decided opinion as to the extent to which the application of manure will be profitable.

The effect of manure on improving the quality of the bark will be considered in the next chapter.

CHAPTER V.

CHEMISTRY OF THE BARK CROP.

WE have now traced to the present time the history of the introduction of medicinal Cinchonas into India and the establishment of plantations of them in this country, and have given some account of the best modes of propagating and cultivating them, but hitherto little allusion has been made to anything concerning the bark—the crop for the sake of which these trees are grown—nor to the modes of harvesting this crop, of improving its constitution, and of extracting the alkaloids which give it its medicinal value.[1] As has been already explained, the medicinal alkaloids contained in bark are Quinine, Cinchonidine, Quinidine, and Cinchonine. A fifth called Aricine is occasionally found, but has never been used in medicine. M. Hesse has also recently announced the existence of another alkaloid occuring only in the *succirubra* barks grown in Sikkim. This base has received the name of Quinamine. As everybody knows, it is the first of these which has hitherto formed the specific for malarious fever. Bark for the manufacture of this alkaloid consequently brings a price in direct proportion to the amount of Quinine contained in it. The barks of *Calisaya*, *officinalis*, and *Pitayensis* contain the largest proportions of Quinine and are consequently the most valuable to a Quinine-maker, who in buying a bark takes account only of the Quinine in it, and allows little or nothing for the other alkaloids. Cinchona barks, however, have long had a recognised value otherwise than as sources of Quinine. They have long been regarded as most valuable tonics, and as such are used for making various pharmaceutical preparations, decoctions, tinctures, &c. For the manufacture of such preparations, Red bark, as being the richest of all in its yield of *total alkaloids*, has always been much esteemed, and of late years (since it began to get scarce) has brought a price as high or even higher than that got for the barks richer in Quinine. The demand, however, for such tonic pharmaceutical preparations being but limited, from the fact that they are chiefly used in Europe, there is no

Relative values of the Cinchona barks.

Red bark chiefly a druggist's bark.

---

[1] From the time when the first Nilgiri trees had become large enough to yield bark fit for analysis and up to the present date, Mr. Howard, the eminent Quinologist, has favoured Government with his advice and assistance in the conduct of the Cinchona experiment. He has in particular made repeated analyses of the various barks. So long ago as 1863, he reported on a specimen bark from a two-year old *succirubra* tree, informing Government that he found in it the same constituents as in Red Bark from South America. In successive years he furnished analyses proving that, as the trees got older, their bark became richer in alkaloid, until they ultimately reached a degree of richness to which American barks rarely attain, and that the barks renewed under moss were the best of their sort that had ever been analysed. Thus Government at every step were assured of the success of their enterprise. Mr. Howard's exertions did not cease with the appointment of a resident Quinologist for the Nilgiri plantations; on the contrary, they are continued to the present time.

CHEMISTRY OF THE BARK CROP.

probability that Red bark will retain its high price in the face of a largely augmented supply. On the other hand, the demand for Quinine is daily increasing, and there is little fear of an increased supply of barks rich in Quinine causing a fall from the present prices of such. It had for many years been suspected that the other alkaloids in which Red bark is so rich are nearly, if not quite, as efficacious febrifuges as Quinine. The settlement of this point naturally demanded attention at an early stage of the Cinchona experiment. In order to settle it by actual trial, a Commission of sixteen medical officers of the Madras Presidency was appointed in 1866 under the presidency of Dr. Shaw, Inspector-General of Hospitals. This Committee was, by order of Her Majesty's Secretary of State for India, supplied from the manufactory of Messrs. Howard and Sons with a quantity of chemically pure sulphate of each of the three alkaloids—Quinidine, Cinchonidine, and Cinchonine. Extended trials were made with these in the most malarious districts of the Presidency, and the finding of the Committee in their preliminary report, dated 28th February 1867,[1] was—

The alkaloids other than Quinine.

Madras Commission to report on.

> "That in recent cases of uncomplicated paroxysmal fever the new alkaloids appeared to most of the medical officers using them, and to most of the members of the Commission, to be quite as efficacious in the curing of fevers as Quinine. . . . The evidence, so far as it has come before the Commission, does not go to shew the superiority of one alkaloid over another. . . . . . The main conclusion which the members of the Commission have derived from the data before them is that the alkaloids, hitherto but little valued in medicine, are scarcely, if at all, inferior as therapeutical agents to Quinine."

The numerical results on which the Commission founded their conclusions are as follows:—

	No. of Cases.	Cured.	Failed.
Treated by Cinchonine	410	400	10
,, Cinchonidine	359	346	13
,, Quinidine	376	365	11

During the succeeding year, the Commission, altered in constitution by the accession of two new members, continued their investigations. Their operations differed, however, from those of the previous year, by the inclusion of chemically pure Sulphate of Quinine amongst the alkaloids tested. The other alkaloids were thus in this second experiment more effectually pitted against Quinine. The total number of fever cases treated by the four alkaloids was [2] 2,472. Of these 2,445 were cures and 27 were failures. The ratio of failure per 1,000 cases treated was found to be as follows:—

	Ratio of failures per 1,000 cases treated.
Chemically pure Sulphate of Quinine	7·092
,, ,, ,, Quinidine	6·024
,, ,, ,, Cinchonidine	9·925
,, ,, ,, Cinchonine	23·255

---

[1] *Parliamentary Returns on East India Cinchona Cultivation*, printed 9th August 1870, p. 108 et seq.
[2] *Cinchona Return* already quoted, p. 159.

This result would shew that Quinidine is rather more effectual than Quinine, and that Cinchonine is less effectual than the other three alkaloids. The conclusion expressed by the Commission is as follows:—

"In regard to the relative effects of the three new alkaloids, and with them chemically pure Sulphate of Quinine, the evidence derived from their use shews that, with the exception of Sulphate of Cinchonine, as already stated, they, in a remarkable degree, so closely resemble each other in therapeutical and physiological action as to render distinctive description of little or no practical utility. In a large proportion of cases in which they were tried, chemically pure Sulphate of Quinine and Sulphates of Quinidine and Cinchonidine appeared to indicate nearly equal febrifuge power, and in equal circumstances their use produced almost the same physiological results. . . . The result confirms the general opinion expressed by the Commission last year, and likewise conclusively established beyond doubt that ordinary Sulphate of Quinidine, chemically pure Sulphate of Quinine and Sulphate of Quinidine, possess equal febrifuge power: that Sulphate of Cinchonidine is only slightly less efficacious, and that Sulphate of Cinchonine, though considerably inferior to the other alkaloids, is notwithstanding a valuable remedial agent in fever."

The Bombay and Bengal Commissions report favourably. Similar Commissions of medical officers of the Bengal and Bombay Presidencies reported substantially to the same effect. The following extract[1] contains the opinion of one of the leading physicians in Bengal on the respective merits of the alkaloids:—

"Since our report, we have received from Dr. Ewart, of the Calcutta Medical College, an account of some experiments with the alkaloids carried out during the month of October 1866. The period was limited and the cases not numerous, but their character was strongly marked in every instance, and the result of treatment well pronounced. Dr. Ewart states his opinion in the following general conclusions which are fully sustained by the facts he adduces:—

"'Sulphate of Quinidine is an excellent antiperiodic in doses of 5 to 20 grains. It is probably not inferior to quinine, and is easily tolerated by the stomach. It is a good bitter tonic in smaller doses, and may be combined with ferruginous medicines. It is less disagreeable to the taste and stomach than Quinine, and its use is not accompanied by the unpleasant effects known as cinchonism.

"'Sulphate of Cinchonidine stands next in antiperiodic power in 10 to 20-grain doses, and as a tonic in smaller quantities it is agreeable to the stomach and is not accompanied by symptoms analogous to cinchonism.

"'Sulphate of Cinchonine is doubtless a powerful antiperiodic in doses of from 10 to 20 grains. The irritability of stomach caused by it is the great objection to its ever taking rank as a substitute for either of the other alkaloids, but it may be obviated by injecting the medicine in solution hypodermically. It is a good tonic in small doses.'

"There is no longer room to doubt that the alkaloids are capable of being generally used with the best effects in India. They have been compared with Quinine, a drug which possesses, more than any other that can be named, the confidence of medical practitioners here; and have been found, by more than one observer, to supplement this sovereign remedy in some of its points of deficiency. The risk attending their use is clearly not greater than in the case of Quinine, nor such as to be in any way deterrent; while the diversities of opinion on their relative usefulness and potency are no more than will be found between opinions concerning any three drugs of the pharmacopœia examined by separate observers."

These results are eminently satisfactory, especially as Red bark, so rich in the alkaloids other than Quinine, is the species which in every part of India has proved the easiest of propagation, the most luxuriant in growth, and the only one which can be grown at all at low levels.

---

[1] *Report of the Committee of Bengal Medical Officers appointed to examine the Properties of the Cinchona Alkaloids, to the Secretary to the Government of India in the Home Department, 1868.*

CHEMISTRY OF THE BARK CROP.

The establishment of the therapeutic excellence of these alkaloids largely increased the value of the Red bark plantations in India, and made much easier of solution the problem of supplying its fever-stricken population with a cheap and effectual febrifuge. In his report to the Government of Madras, written after his second visit to India in 1865-66, Mr. Markham had directed the special attention of Government to the importance of finding out as soon as possible the best way of dealing with the anticipated produce of the Government plantations so as to secure the avowed

Object of Government in introducting Cinchona into India. object of Government in undertaking the cultivation at all. Had pecuniary profit been that object, it would probably have been best secured by arranging to send the bark to England for sale, and by continuing to purchase Quinine in the usual way, trusting to reduce its price by increasing the supply of bark. But it is extremely doubtful whether, under such an arrangement, a cheap febrifuge would ever have been brought within the reach of fever patients so poor as the agricultural population of India—a population who for ages accustomed to look on often-recurring fever as part of their fate, have become too apathetic to be prepared to pay much for relief from it. The object of Government is that an efficient febrifuge shall be available by purchase in every corner of India, that it shall become part of the stock-in-trade of every village shop-keeper, and that it shall be purchaseable at not more than a rupee an ounce. At the present moment Quinine is available by purchase only in a few of the larger towns where there is a European population, and even in such places it costs from six to ten rupees per ounce. It is of course supplied to all Government dispensaries, but only to a very limited extent, the supply for a year being as a rule really equal to the actual demands of but a few days. The dispensing of so costly and scarce a drug gives rise, it is believed, to much sharp practice among the lower officials at dispensaries and hospitals, and a dose of the coveted febrifuge is probably as a rule unattainable to the very poorest of the patients.

Mr. Markham's suggestions as to the utilisation of Indian Cinchona barks. Mr. Markham suggested that, instead of sending the bark to England to be sold, a febrifuge should be prepared from it at the Government plantations which should contain the alkaloids in a rough form and should be saleable at a cheap rate. He recommended the preparation called Quinium, a product which (while an effectual febrifuge) would not be bought up by speculators as a source of Quinine, it being unsaleable for manufacturing purposes. Quinium is made by treating pounded bark with slaked lime and the resulting lime product with alcohol. Mr.

Mr. Markam recommends the appointment of a Quinologist. Markham considered that a competent chemist should be got from England and located on the Nilgiris whose functions should be to work out the whole subject of Indian Quinology. His recommendation coincided with others which had been made to the same effect, and was subsequently strengthened by the verdict of the Alkaloid Commissions already referred to. Accordingly, in October 1866, the Secretary of State appointed as Government Quinologist on the Nilgiris

Mr. Broughton's appointment. Mr. John Broughton, then Dr. Frankland's Assistant at the Royal Institution, London. Mr. Broughton was engaged for a period of three years, and his duties were defined as follows: to discover by repeated analyses of bark from plants growing in different situations, the conditions as regards elevation, climate, soil, and exposure best calculated to produce the largest possible yield of alkaloids; to ascertain the difference as regards yield and efficiency between green and dried barks; to analyse the leaves and flowers of the different species; to settle the best method of drying the bark; and finally, to enable Her Majesty's Government to arrive at a decision with respect to the best and cheapest method of preparing the febrifuge for use among the poorer classes of the natives of India. Mr. Broughton arrived at Ootacamund in January 1867 and decided to build his analytical laboratory there: his alkaloid manufactory, however, was subsequently established at Neddiwattum. Mr. Broughton's attention was at first of course directed to an analysis of the barks yielded on the plantation, and in April 1867 he published his first report, giving results confirmatory of those previously obtained by Mr. Howard. Since his appointment, Mr. Broughton has worked steadily towards the ends set before him by the Secretary of State, and has published his results in a series of able and interesting reports communicated to the Madras Government, and in some papers laid before the Royal Society of London. These results may now be roughly summarised. They are as follows [1]:—

(1) The leaves of Cinchona contain but a minute quantity of alkaloid, and only about half of that is quinine. So far back as the year 1863, the late Dr. Anderson concluded, as the result of some experiments made at Darjeeling, that the leaves contain some alkaloids, and he believed that they might be of value as a febrifuge. This hope is dispelled by Mr. Broughton, who has determined the amount to be as follows:—

Cinchona leaves contain little alkaloid.

	Total Alkaloids.	Quinine.
In dried leaves of Red bark	0·0190	0·008
In dried leaves of Crown or Pale bark	0·0111	0·005

The bitter taste of the leaves is largely due to the presence of Quinine.

(2) The flowers of the cinchonas contain no alkaloid but a considerable amount of quinovine; while ripening fruit contains but the faintest trace of alkaloid, and ripe seed none whatever. The act of flowering does not appear to have any direct influence on the amount of alkaloid in the bark.

Cinchona flowers contain no alkaloid.

(3) As regards the wood of cinchona trees, Mr. Broughton found that dry Red bark wood contains 0·08 to 0·11 per cent. of alkaloid, of which 0·004 is quinine, and that Pale or Crown bark wood yields 0·0101 per cent., with 0·004 of quinine.

Cinchona wood contains little alkaloid.

---

[1] Parliamentary Return, *East India Cinchona Cultivation*, printed 9th August 1870, pp. 237 *et seq.*

CHEMISTRY OF THE BARK CROP.

(4) The order in which the alkaloids are formed in the bark of living trees appears to be as follows: The first to appear is one which resembles quinine in every respect except in not forming crystallisable salts. This alkaloid is found alike in the original bark of young trees, and in strips of young bark forming over the cambium of old trees to replace strips of the original bark which have been removed. The chemical changes which occur in the bark are thus related more to the age of the bark than to the age of the tree. As time passes on, this primitive alkaloid resembling quinine becomes replaced partly by real crystallisable quinine (the desideratum of the quinine manufacturer) and partly by cinchonidine. Although Mr. Broughton has never actually succeeded in converting quinine into cinchonidine by artificial means, he is led to believe that such a transmutation occurs in nature. This conclusion is supported by many collateral facts.

The order in which the alkaloids are formed in cinchona bark.

(5) High temperature favours the formation of cinchonidine and diminishes that of quinine. Bark of trees grown at a low elevation, and of those grown even at a high elevation but of which the stems have been exposed to sun-light, contains a large proportion of cinchonidine, and is *pro tanto* poor in quinine. A low mean temperature, within certain limits, is therefore favourable to the production of quinine. Deprivation of light favours the increase of the total amount of alkaloids in a bark. Mr. Broughton covered the stem of a cinchona tree with a shield of tinned plate and the stem of another with black cloth, his object being to keep the bark in darkness without impeding the access of air or protecting it from the heating influence of the sun's rays. The results were that, after ten month's protection in this way, the amount of total alkaloids was found to be increased by about 2·8 per cent. in each case.

High temperature unfavourable to formation of Quinine.

(6) The researches of Mr. J. E. Howard and of Dr. Flückiger, confirmed by those of Mr. Broughton, prove that the alkaloids are contained in the outer and cellular portion of the bark, and not in the inner, fibrous or liber layer, and it even appears that an increased development of the fibrous part of a bark is accompanied by a decrease in the amount of quinine in it.

Cellular tissue the seat of the alkaloids.

(7) Intimately connected with the last two results is the fact, first brought into prominence by the result of Mr. McIvor's experiments, that bark renewed under moss contains a larger amount of both total and crystallisable alkaloids than ordinary bark. Such bark is more cellular than ordinary bark, and has, by means of the moss, to a great extent been protected both from the heat and light of the sun's rays during its formation.

Renewed bark rich in crystallisable alkaloids.

(8) The alkaloids in living Red bark are not permanent in either nature or quantity. On the contrary, they are affected both by the seasons of the year and also by age. During the rainy season on the Nilgiris (from June to September) the yield of total alkaloids is at its lowest. It rises at the end of the rains (*i. e.*, towards the latter half of September) and continues high during the cold and dry weather, falling slightly

Alkaloids in living bark not permanent.

during February and March, rising again in April, and attaining its maximum in May. The yield of crystallisable sulphates in the main follows a similar line of variation. The dry season is, therefore, other things being equal, the time to collect bark. The particular part of the dry season must, however, in some measure be influenced by the readiness or the reverse with which the bark can be separated from the wood. The seasonal variation in crown bark has not been determined.

(9) The chemical form or state of combination in which the alkaloids occur in living bark is a point of much importance. Mr. Broughton's researches lead him to believe that, in red bark, four-fifths of the total amount of alkaloids exist combined with Quino-tannic acid in a *solid* state within the tissues, and most probably exclusively within the cellular tissue. The alkaloids appear not to be very active vital constituents, but rather to be stores "of which only a small portion at the most shares in the changes incident to growth." The remaining fifth of the total alkaloid is in solution in the juice of the bark.

The salts formed by the alkaloids in living bark.

(10) Up to a certain point in the life of a Red bark tree the total alkaloids contained in its bark increase in quantity, the annual increments diminishing in amount until a maximum is reached. The proportion of crystallisable quinine, however, rather diminishes as the maximum yield of total alkaloids is approached. The maximum of total alkaloids is reached about the ninth year, after which age not only waste but deterioration begins, the total amount of alkaloid diminishing and cinchonidine becoming transformed into Cinchonine—an alkaloid of less value. The influence of age on the Crown barks has, owing to their great variability in quality at all ages, not been settled with the same degree of certainty, but it is probably less than in the case of Red bark.

Proportion of alkaloids varies with age.

(11) One of the most important conclusions arrived at by Mr. Broughton is that "the most vigorous and rapidly growing tress yield a much richer bark than more stunted and less vigorous trees of the same age, and of course they yield at the same time more bark." Hence, whatever conditions stimulate growth have a direct effect in increasing the yield of alkaloid. The bark of diseased trees contains little alkaloid and that of dead trees none whatever.

The most healthy trees yield the richest bark.

(12) Mr. Broughton's experiments shew that Red bark is but little benefited by the application of manure, the increase in alkaloid resulting from its application being but slight, and little of that increase being Quinine. Crown bark, on the other hand, was found to be much improved by manuring. An application of farm-yard manure three or four times during a period of about five years gave an increase in pure quinine of 4·75 per cent., and in total alkaloids of 2·81 per cent., thus raising the value of the bark about half-a-crown a pound. A pound of guano given to a tree caused an increase of total alkaloids in the bark of 2·5 per cent., of which 2 per cent. was quinine, thus raising the value of its bark eighteen pence a pound. Ammonia Sulphate in doses of ¾ lb. per tree gave an increase of 1·22 per cent. of total alkaloids and of 0·57 per cent. of quinine. A curious point in this

Effects of manure on composition of bark.

experiment was that none of these manures caused any apparent increased growth of the trees, and did not even affect the tint of their foliage.

(13) Mr. Broughton's elaborate experiments on different modes of drying bark prove that exposure to a high temperature, especially in a moist atmosphere, causes an alteration in the chemical composition of the alkaloids and renders bark almost worthless. Even the sun's rays are hurtful if bark is long exposed to them. To secure it in the best possible condition, bark should be taken off the trees in large pieces, and these should be arranged on drying stages, under shelter from the light and heat of the sun's rays, but open to the access of air. The pieces should be frequently turned. Bark should be taken off in dry weather only. If allowed to become mouldy and to ferment, as is apt to happen if it be taken during wet weather, deterioration more or less serious surely occurs. Dry bark, on the other hand, will keep unchanged for many months.

Modes of drying bark.

(14) Mr. Broughton calculates[1] that trunk bark loses from 70 to 74·8 per cent. of weight in drying, and branch bark from 75 to 76 per cent. The Sikkim experience goes to shew that trunk red bark loses 73 per cent. and twig bark 75 per cent.

Loss of weight in bark by drying.

Such are the facts in the life-history and chemistry of the Cinchona alkaloids which Mr. Broughton has elicited and determined.

---

[1] *Report to Secretary to Government of Madras*, dated 1st December 1873, Appendix.

CHAPTER VI.

MODE OF HARVESTING THE BARK CROP.

Two matters of practical importance still remain to be discussed, and to these the remaining chapters of this report will be devoted. These matters are, *first*, the most profitable means of harvesting the bark crop; *second*, the best means of extracting the alkaloids contained in it, so as to obtain the largest amount of an effectual febrifuge at the least possible cost. Mr. McIvor's attention was early directed to the solution of the problem of how to produce the greatest amount of alkaloid in the least amount of time. From the beginning he appears to have been full of faith that, under cultivation, the total yield of alkaloid and the proportionate amount of Quinine in any bark could be increased. In April 1863 he reported to Government that "the Cinchona tree has the power of rapidly renewing its bark, if the spaces from which the latter is taken are immediately covered with damp moss;" and that the new bark formed over these spaces is thicker, in proportion, than that part of the bark which had not been interfered with. Subsequent experience led Mr. McIvor to the double conclusion that not only can the amount of bark yielded by a tree be very much increased by the process of mossing, but that the total amount of alkaloids (and especially the proportion of crystallisable Quinine) in bark so renewed is considerably greater than in natural bark. Mr. McIvor proposed to harvest all Cinchona bark in this way, and in 1865 he sought to obtain a patent for his method, so as to secure to himself a pecuniary interest in its application. This was, however, disallowed. Mr. McIvor's mossing process is thus described in his own words[1]:—

Renewal under moss.

"A labourer proceeds to an eight-year old tree, and, reaching up as far as he can, makes a horizontal incision of the required width. From either end of this incision he runs a vertical incision to the ground, and then, carefully raising with his knife the bark at the horizontal incision until he can seize it with his fingers, he strips off the bark to the ground and cuts it off. The strip of bark then presents the appearance of a ribbon more or less long. Supposing the tree to be of 28 inches in circumference, the labourer will take nine of the above ribbons, each 1¼ inches wide. He will thus leave, after the tree has been stripped, other nine ribbons still adhering to the tree, each somewhat broader than the stripped ribbon and at intervals apart, occupied by the spaces to which the stripped ribbons had adhered. As soon as he has removed his strips, the labourer will proceed to moss the trunk all round, tying on the moss with some fibre. The decorticated intervals will thus be excluded from light and air, and this point is one of the capital points in the system. The mere exclusion of light and air from a stem partially bared of bark acts in two ways: it enables a healing process to be rapidly set up in the same way as a plaster does in the case of a wound in an animal organism: and it has this further curious effect—it increases the secretion of Quinine in the bark renewed under its protection. This increase of Quinine is admitted by Mr. Broughton in all his reports. At the end of six or twelve months the bands of bark left untouched at the first stripping are removed, and the intervals they occupied on the trunk are mossed. At the end of twenty-two months, on an

Description of the process of mossing.

---

[1] *Report to the Commissioner of the Nilgiris*, dated 9th August 1873.

MODE OF HARVESTING THE BARK CROP.

average, the spaces occupied by the ribbons originally taken are found to be covered with renewed bark much thicker than the natural bark of the same age, and this renewed bark can be removed and a fresh process of renewal again be fostered by moss. In another six or twelve months, the renewed bark of the natural ribbons left at the first stripping can be taken and so on; harvests are obtainable from the trunk, alternately from the spaces left at the first stripping and the spaces left by the second stripping. Experience hitherto does not shew any limit to the taking of these harvests from a tree. Of course, it is understood that at every stripping the ribbons taken are longer than at the preceding stripping, because the tree has each year increased in height and bulk, and, therefore, the top of every ribbon consists of natural bark and the lower part of renewed bark." Mr. McIvor farther adds, "All experience hitherto acquired shews that bark invariably renews. It renews easily and early when the cambium is untouched. In cases where the cambium is injured, the renewal proceeds, but the process is slower. In respect of universal renewal, there is no difference whatever between the Red and Crown barks."

Arguments in favour of, and against, mossing.

Mr. McIvor has all along urged that this mode of cultivating and cropping bark will be found by far more profitable than any other. Its advantages, as stated by him, are—that, as the bark (if taken with proper precautions) is almost invariably renewed by the end of periods varying from twelve to twenty-two months, a crop, amounting to half the trunk bark of a tree and increasing in actual amount *pari passu* with the growth of the latter, can be regularly taken about once a year without in any way interfering with the health and vigour of the tree; and, moreover, that the bark so taken is richer in total alkaloids, and specially richer in crystallisable Quinine, than natural bark. By following this plan Mr. McIvor believes that advantage can always be taken of the period in its growth when renewed bark is richest in alkaloid, so that it may be removed then. This is on the supposition that at that period the bark shall have attained sufficient thickness, which of course it may not have done. Mr. Broughton's more recent investigations on the effects of mossing Red bark go to shew that the increase of total alkaloid, which undoubtedly characterises renewed bark on young trees, does not characterise the renewed bark of trees which have arrived at the age of maximum yield,—in other words that, on trees more than eight years old, moss-renewed bark is not richer, as far as yield of total alkaloid is concerned, than natural bark of the same age. Such bark appears, however, to contain more crystallisable Quinine than natural bark and is thus more valuable as a source of pure Quinine, although not more so as a source of Cinchona alkaloid. It must not be forgotten that mossing deals with only part of the bark of a tree, namely, half or third of that covering the trunk. Mr. Broughton's most recent inference from his analyses is therefore, if correct, of some importance. It is to the effect that there is apparently a transference of alkaloid from the untouched, into the renewing, bark, and that, therefore, if the renewed mossed bark of a tree be enriched, the natural bark remaining on the same tree above the region treated by moss is *pro tanto* impoverished. Mr. Broughton has recently been farther led to conclude that the renewal of bark is not by any means an invariable result of treatment with moss. On the contrary, he estimated that 85 per cent. of 2,000 trees barked and mossed in 1871 had, two years later, either wholly or partially failed to renew their bark. This conclusion was substantially confirmed by Dr. Bidie, who was sent to report specially on the subject. These 2,000 trees are, however, stated by Mr. McIvor to have been barked and mossed by unskilled labour: moreover, Mr. McIvor maintains that their failure to renew their bark has been much exaggerated.

Additional serious objections to the mossing system are, the necessity (in order to prevent injury to the delicate cambium,[1]) of having the operation done by skilled and careful men under constant European supervision, the fact that, at the age when it is richest in alkaloids, the renewed bark is frequently found to be much thinner than natural bark, and the consequent necessity of allowing it to stand until it thickens, thus reducing the frequency of cropping from once in eighteen months (as originally estimated by Mr. McIvor) to once in from two to three years, and finally the diminution in health[2] and vigour actually observed in trees which have been submitted to the process—a diminution so great as to involve the danger of their premature death. As already explained, bark is only successfully renewed when it is formed regularly over the entire surface of the wood that has been laid bare. If the delicate cambium surface has been injured by rough handling, the damaged part of the wood dies; it does not reproduce bark, and, unless covered by lateral growth from the cut edge of the natural bark, it remains bare. The bare part ultimately decays, and thus disease is introduced into the stem.

The minor objections to the process are, that it can be done only when there is much moisture in the air, and that consequently bark must be harvested at the very seasons when it is most difficult to dry it for exportation; and that, even if wet bark is to be used for local manufacture, the supplies are poured into the factory during a limited season of the year only.

Mossing a failure in Sikkim. — Mossing has been tried in the Sikkim plantations and has totally failed from a cause not alluded to in any of the Nilgiri reports,—namely, the attacks of ants. In every tree treated by Mr. McIvor's process in Sikkim, the renewing bark has, as fast as formed, been regularly eaten by these insects, to which the moss apparently forms a most acceptable cover, and to which the succulent young-bark cells appear to afford a particularly attractive food. This is no matter of surmise or theory, for these insects have repeatedly been observed at work by Mr. Gammie, the resident manager of the plantation, and also by myself. Trees covered with straw, instead of moss, fared no better.

Renewal of bark without moss. — A number of trees, however, which were recently barked in Sikkim in the way described by Mr. McIvor, but which were left bare of any kind of covering whatever, have renewed their bark fairly well, the

---

[1] On this point Dr. Bidie in his report to the Government of Madras, dated 13th November 1873, writes:—

"It is of great importance that the cambium layer should not be injured by the knife, or be allowed to dry, or be exposed to the sun, as, if injured in any of these ways, the bark will fail to renew."

[2] Dr. Bidie's testimony regarding this is as follows:—

"So far as mere dimensions of stem go, there is but little difference between the mossed and unmossed (Red bark) trees; but, taking a bird's-eye view of the trees, the most casual observer cannot fail to notice the superior luxuriance of the unmossed."

And again, concerning the Crown barks, he writes:—

"The mossed Crown barks, owing to the renewal of their lower branches and the faded hue of their foliage, present, on taking a bird's-eye view of an estate, a very inferior appearance compared with trees that have not been barked. I also observed, in both the Red and Crown barks which had been mossed, a tendency to produce an unusual amount of flower and seed—a peculiarity very common in plants which may have had their vitality reduced in any way."

MODE OF HARVESTING THE BARK CROP.

renewal taking place (as in successful mossing) not by growth from the edges of the bark left on the stem, but by development over the entire denuded cambium surface. The bark thus renewed has not yet been submitted to analysis, being as yet not sufficiently old to be judged of. The successful renewal of Cinchona bark without protection has also been observed in the Nilgiri plantations.[1]

Coppicing: description of the process. The other system by which it has been proposed to take the bark crop on the Nilgiris is that known as coppicing. This consists in cutting down trees either close to the ground or within a short distance of it, and of allowing one or more of the crop of shoots which rises from the stumps to grow. If any shoots naturally arise from near the base of the stem prior to cutting it, these would of course be left to form coppice, instead of trusting to the formation of entirely new shoots from the cut stump. As a fact, such natural root-shoots do not occur to any great extent on healthy Cinchona trees at Sikkim, although they appear to do so in the Nilgiris. Coppicing is a mode of working well known in forestry and is done in several ways; thus, the trees in a piece of forest may be cut down all at once; or a proportion only may be felled, leaving the young shoots originating from their stumps to grow under the protection of the larger trees left standing. One or other of these modes is that proposed as an alternative to mossing. If Mr. Broughton is correct as to the period of the maximum richness of Red bark, and if it be desired to take advantage of that period, the trees would, under the coppicing system, be felled during the eighth year of their age; and from the stumps two or three shoots would be allowed to grow, which shoots would in turn be felled (when of sufficient size) either simultaneously, or one at a time annually until all are cut. The cutting of each shoot would be followed by the appearance of new shoots from the stump. A steady, successive series of crops of bark could, it is believed, thus be got from a plantation treated coppice-fashion. That other trees continue to yield coppice for a long series of years is a well-known fact of which the extensive hard-wood coppices of France and Germany, and the Cinnamon coppices of Ceylon, need only be mentioned as instances. It seems pretty well established that in their natural forests on the Andes, Cinchona trees sprout freely from their cut stumps. The presumptions in favour of the success of coppicing appear therefore pretty strong. It is much to be regretted that hitherto treatment of Cinchonas coppice-fashion has received no proper trial in the Nilgiris, whereas many thousand trees have been submitted to the mossing process. Mr. McIvor's return of coppiced trees is as follows:—

Experience of coppicing in the Nilgiris.

There were coppiced in December 1866 about 50 trees.
                in January 1867 „ 50 „
                in May 1871 „ 240 „
                in June 1873 „ 58 „
                in October 1873 „ 57 „

                    Total   ... 455 trees.

---

[1] See Dr. Bidie's report, paragraph 16.

Of these, he informs us, a considerable percentage died after being cut (that is, they sent up no new shoots), and the shoots of those that survived were but poor. Mr. McIvor speaks of the shoots on some trees at Neddiwuttum as being when seven years old "mere wands" clothed with bark " too thin to be of any value whatever." In his report already alluded to, Dr. Bidie gives his opinion of the Nilgiri coppicing experiments in the following words:—

"So far we may be said to have had in the Nilgiris no experience whatever of this method of harvesting the bark, as the few experiments which have been made have been on too small a scale, and not conducted in a manner likely to throw much light on the subject. The oldest coppiced trees are some Red barks which were cut down in 1866. I was not able to find the whole of these, but those which I saw had not done well. This is hardly to be wondered at, as, in the first place, some of the trees were immediately over the scrap of a road,—a bad situation for coppiced trees,—and, in the next place, too many shoots had been left to grow up from the stumps. The coppicing experiment was made in 1871, 240 $C.$ *succirubra* trees having been cut down in that year. Of these, 40 are on the Kilgraston estate and form a single row, flanked on each side by tall neighbours; while the 200 are on the Denison estate and constitute a plot which has been completely cleared. As regards the 40 trees on the Kilgraston estate, they can hardly be said to have had fair play, as their neighbours have so completely shaded them as to deprive them, to a considerable extent, of the necessary light and air. Too many shoots have also been allowed to spring up from the stools, and these shoots, owing to the dense shade, were observed, in many instances, to be too feeble to stand erect. No opinion as to coppicing can be deduced from this part of the experiment. The 200 coppiced trees on the Denison estate have done better, all the stools, with a very few exceptions, having survived, and the shoots have grown fairly and are looking healthy.

"Another coppicing experiment was carried out in June 1873, 58 Red bark trees having been cut down, while a similar number of contiguous trees, of the same species and age, were barked and mossed with the view of the results of the two systems being rigidly contrasted. I must say at once that this trial is on much too paltry a scale, and that the coppiced trees were cut at an unfortunate period of the year, as, being then full of sap, they of course bled profusely and thus ran a great risk of dying or having their vitality more or less permanently impaired. Owing to the short time that had elapsed since this experiment was instituted, it was quite useless for any practical deductions; but I may remark that all the stools had either thrown up shoots or gave promise of doing so. The same remarks apply to a small coppicing experiment on Crown barks on the Dodabetta estate, those trees having also been cut in June 1873."

Objections to coppicing.

The objections urged against the application of coppicing to Cinchonas may be summed up as follows:—

1st.—The stump of the felled tree (usually called *the stool*) may fail to send up shoots. This not unfrequently happens, even with healthy trees, both in the Nilgiris and in Sikkim. In the case of unhealthy trees the results are of course much less favourable.

The stools may fail to shoot.

2nd.—It has been urged that coppicing is a difficult and delicate operation. On the Continent of Europe and in England no such difficulty is experienced, and coppicing is done by unskilled labour. In Sikkim, ordinary hill coolies of by no means great intelligence are found to do it quite well. The thinning-out of the shoots that spring from the stool, so as to leave only two or three of the best of

It is said to be a difficult and delicate operation.

MODE OF HARVESTING THE BARK CROP.

them, is the most delicate operation connected with coppicing; yet this is found in Sikkim to be a task which a coolie of ordinary intelligence can be taught in a few lessons.

3rd.—It has been said that coppice shoots grow more slowly than young trees. In Sikkim four-year old *succirubra* trees average in height 15 feet: four-year old shoots from the stools of trees cut at the age of four years average 12·4 feet in height. Such shoots are not, however, so thick as the stems of untouched four-year old trees.

Coppice shoots said to grow slowly.

4th.—The bark of coppiced shoots is said to be thin and worthless. Mr. Broughton's and Mr. Wood's analyses of such bark yield results which shew it to be as good as, if not better than, original bark.

Coppice bark said to be thin and worthless.

5th.—It has also been given as an objection to coppice that, as the removal of the shade of the older trees is rapidly followed by a growth of weeds, the annual cost of keeping it clear of weeds will be about equal to that of keeping up a young plantation. The weight of this objection has, however, been rather exaggerated, for it is found that, if only alternate rows of old trees, or if alternate trees in alternate rows, be cut, sufficient shade is given by the heads of the trees left standing, not only to protect the young stool-shoots, but also to a great extent to keep weeds in check. It is, moreover, doubtful whether the total abandonment of all cultivation, although a cheap, is really a desirable or profitable policy; for it must be remembered that Cinchona trees of all ages receive much benefit from the moderate stirring of the soil that is incidental to the operations of weeding and hoeing.

Said to be an expensive method.

6th.—It is very strongly insisted on both by Mr. McIvor[1] and by the Commissioner of the Nilgiris that more bark can be taken from a tree within a given time by mossing than by coppicing.' An illustration is given by the latter as follows[2]:—

Said to yield less bark than the mossing process.

"One thousand *succirubra* trees of eight years old were mossed. They will be twelve years old in September next. In these four years they have given at four harvestings—

        2,980 ℔s in 1871-72 of dry bark.
          764 ,, ,, 1872-73 ,,
        1,546 ,, ,, 1873-74 ,,
          770 ,, ,, 1874-75 ,,

        6,060 ,,

or in all 6,000 and odd pounds of dry bark. On the other hand, the 240 trees coppiced by my predecessor and Mr. Broughton in May 1871 gave the following results: 200

---
[1] Letter from Mr. McIvor to the Commissioner of the Nilgiris, dated 9th August 1873.
[2] Letter from the Commissioner of the Nilgiris, to the Secretary to the Government of Madras, dated 17th June 1874, paragraph 17.

of the trees were coppiced in one block. They were of the season 1862-63. The other 40 trees were of the season 1864-65, and they were coppiced in alternate rows. The bark obtained from the 240 trees aggregated 720 lbs. of green trunk bark (equal to 255 lbs. of dry bark) and 324 lbs. of green branch bark (equal to 100 lbs. of dry bark). The whole quantity of dry bark attained was thus 355 lbs., or 1·48 lb. per tree. I have on several occasions stated that these trees have given nothing since. Therefore the mossed trees have yielded 6 lbs. of dry bark per tree against 1·48 lb. in the case of the coppiced trees, including all the branch bark, which of course has not been taken in the mossed trees. Six pounds each tree of mossed trunk bark have to be set against 1½ lb. of mixed trunk and branch bark, or four times the quantity of the more valuable bark."

The figures just quoted would seem to shew a strong case in favour of mossing. It must not, however, be forgotten that, whereas the mossing experiments were conducted with much enthusiasm and care, those in coppicing were on a very small scale, received but little attention, and are admitted by everybody to have been inadequate and unsatisfactory. These figures are, moreover, vitiated for the purposes of comparison by an obvious, though doubtless unintentional error. The 1,000 trees referred to as mossed were eight years old; they yielded[1] in 1871-72, 2,980 lbs. of dry bark per tree. But this was *natural* bark, originally covering their stems, which was taken off to allow moss to be applied, and it is equal to about three pounds per tree. Of the six pounds claimed as the produce of these mossed trees, half the quantity is thus original bark which existed on them prior to the application of moss, the other half is bark renewed under moss. On the other hand, the 240 coppiced trees were, as Mr. McIvor states,[2] of two ages; 200 were eight years old and 40 were five and a half years old. They yielded only 1·48 lb. of original bark (the bark of both stem and branches being included), and must therefore have been very much smaller trees than the thousand which yielded, *from their stems only*, three pounds each of original bark. The bark of the four-year old shoots of these coppiced trees is, besides, not calculated at all. In Sikkim we know that the value of bark taken from four-year old coppice shoots rising from stools from 5½ to 8 years old would be considerable.

The two systems compared.
The contrast between the Nilgiri results of mossing as compared to coppicing, imperfect although the latter are, is therefore not so great as at first sight appears.

But, even accepting Mr. McIvor's estimate of the yield obtainable by mossing, it does not appear that the data as to the comparative merits of the two systems are as yet sufficient to warrant the formation of a final and definite opinion as to which is the preferable one in practice for the Nilgiris. It may possibly be found that a compromise may be most advantageous, and that it may pay best first to take a crop of bark by mossing and then to coppice the trees. The removal of a large part of the bark of a tree every year can hardly fail to cause an amount of derangement in its vital processes which can scarcely be beneficial to its health. It will not therefore be anticipated by anybody at all conversant with vegetable physiology or with practical horticulture, that Cinchona trees will for a long series of years not only bear annual decortication with impunity, but go on producing, with the regularity of machines, annual crops of bark of high quality. Ex-

---

[1] See Mr. McIvor's annual report on the Nilgiri Cinchona Plantations for 1871-72, paragraph 11.
[2] Letter to Commissioner of the Nilgiris, dated August 1873.

perience alone will decide how long they will live under such treatment. It has already taught that on the Nilgiris the trees will do for sometime,[1] and the supporters of mossing say for long enough time to yield better results than any other mode of bark harvest hitherto proposed. It is urged by the advocates of the process that, if mossed trees shew symptoms of failing health, they can be coppiced or replaced by seedlings, and that, even under these circumstances, they will have paid better than had they been coppiced.

Experience of coppicing in Sikkim.
With the view of estimating the merits of the coppicing system, a number of trees of various ages were cut down in the Sikkim plantation towards the end of the year 1874. About a year later (*i. e.*, in September 1875) these plants were examined and the details of the measurements of the coppice of a few of them may here be given in a tabular form.[2] The figures are as follows:—

Number of plants measured.	When planted.	Planting distance.	When coppiced.	Percentage of plants which have failed to send up shoots from their stools and which are presumably dead.	Percentage of plants in which the coppice shoots are two or more.	Average height of coppice in September 1875.	Remarks.
						Feet.	
50	1866	6×6 feet	Dec. 1870	12	...	12·4	
100	1866	Ditto	,, 1874	7	26 per cent.	2·58	From this patch a few cankered plants had been cut and some thinning of healthy trees had been done between 1870 and 1873. In 1874 a patch was cut down almost entirely, a few trees only being left per acre. The measurements here given are those therefore of as nearly as may be a clean coppice, free from shade.
50	1867	Ditto	,, 1874	2	57 ,,	2·68	
20	1867	Ditto	,, 1874	5	...	2·20	The trees were cut in rows in the plantation, the coppice was therefore shaded.
100	1867	Ditto	,, 1874	23	31 per cent.	2·70	Ditto ditto.
100	1868	Ditto	,, 1874	18	34 ,,	2·46	Ditto ditto.
20	1869	Ditto	Nov. 1874	10	None	2·35	Ditto ditto.
100	1870	Ditto	Dec. 1874	30	71 per cent.	3·34	Ditto ditto.
86	1871	Ditto	,, 1874	17	61 ,,	3·91	Ditto ditto.
100	1872	4×4	,, 1874	36	20 ,,	3·27	The trees in this patch were very vigorous and had large shady heads. The coppice therefore was smothered.—See remarks on page 66.

---

[1] It is quite beside the question to quote, as has been done, the repeated and long-continued yield of cork by the cork-oak and to argue from that in favour of the success of continued artificial decortication of Cinchona trees. Cork consists of the outer bark, which, when not removed artificially, is shed spontaneously by the trees at stated intervals. The inner bark of the tree forms no part of the *cork* of commerce, and neither in the artificial removal nor in the natural shedding of cork is the inner bark layer removed. The young wood or cambium is therefore never exposed. Medicinal Cinchona bark, on the contrary, consists of the entire bark, outer as well as inner; and, in the process of mossing, the whole is removed and the young wood or cambium is laid bare—a process to which there is nothing analogous in the collection of cork. The habit of naturally shedding the outer bark is not peculiar to the cork-oak, but occurs in other plants. As familiar examples, may be mentioned the grape-vine and the guava.

[2] The measurements of the coppice shoots of fifty trees planted in 1866 and cut down in December 1870 are also given.

These figures give a fair example of the condition of some thousands of coppiced trees in the Sikkim plantation : they cannot on the whole be regarded as very favourable. One important item of the Sikkim experience of coppice is that shoots grown under shade are inclined to be thin and lank, and they are undoubtedly less healthy and vigorous than those of the coppice that follows a complete, or nearly complete, clearance of the old trees. The expense of keeping such a coppice clear of weeds is, as has been already pointed out, considerable.

It must be admitted that we are still ignorant of one most important fact in Cinchona cultivation in India, and one which has a most important bearing on modes of taking the bark crop; the fact is this—*we do not know the age to which the trees will naturally live in this country*. If their lives are to be short, it will be advisable to adopt working plans involving early taking of the bark; if they are to be long-lived, longer-deferred cropping must be practised. With regard to mixed coppice, we do not know exactly up to what age the shade of the older trees is advantageous or the reverse to the young shoots. There is, doubtless, a period at which the shade of the older trees will begin to be disadvantageous to the coppice under them, and, as soon as this period arrives, the older trees must be sufficiently thinned out. Recent analyses by Mr. Wood, the Government Quinologist on the Sikkim plantation, go to shew that the yield of alkaloid is really not so much affected in Sikkim by the age of the tree as Mr. Broughton found it to be in the Nilgiris; and that the bark of healthy trees from four to eight [1] years old, and of coppice shoots from three to four years old, is all pretty much the same in its percentage of total alkaloid. Mr. Wood is further inclined to think that, at all ages of the trees, the

---

[1] The following extract from Mr. Wood's report to the Bengal Government, dated 24th May 1875, contains some analyses of *succirubra* stem bark of various ages :—

"The next point for consideration is the alkaloidal value of the bark. Wishing in the first place to ascertain the maximum quality to which our *succirubra* attains, and having already examined bark taken from trees growing at different elevations, I requested Mr. Gammie to obtain for me samples from the stems of our finest trees of different ages. He therefore furnished me with seven samples.

"The results of analysis were as follows :—

				Total Alkaloid.
No. I, trees planted in 1866				6·7 per cent.
,, II ,,	,,	,, 1867		7·3 ,,
,, III ,,	,,	,, 1868		6·8 ,,
,, IV ,,	,,	,, 1869		6·81 ,,
,, V ,,	,,	,, 1870		6·63 ,,
,, VI ,,	,,	,, 1871		6·04 ,,
,, VII ,,	,,	,, 1872		7·68 ,,

"The constituents of the total alkaloid from the oldest and youngest of these were determined :—

	No. 1. (1866).	No. 6. (1871).	No. 7. (1872).
"Total alkaloid	6·7	6·04	7·08
Alkaloid soluble in Ether	2·4	2·73	2·17
Cinchonidine	1·9	1·99	2·95
Cinchonine	2·4	1·31	2·56
Crystalline Sulphate of Quinine	1·3	1·35	·82

"The mixed stem and branch bark of *succirubra* trees of similar ages gave the following result :—

	Total Alkaloid.
"1866	4·37 per cent."
1867	5·10 ,,
1868	4·85 ,,
1869	4·32 ,,
1870	4·85 ,,
1871	4·80 ,,
1872	4·23 ,,

MODE OF HARVESTING THE BARK CROP.

value of bark depends on its position on the stem, the richest stem bark being nearest the base of the stem, and the poorest nearest its apex, the bark of the larger roots being the richest of all and that of the small branches the poorest. The first of these discoveries has an important bearing on the question of bark harvesting, and makes it highly probable that, if the object be to grow bark for the sake of its total alkaloid (and this is the avowed object of Government), and not merely for its Quinine, it will probably pay best to plant thickly,[1] as in Sikkim, and to take the crop early. By plant-

Modifications of coppic-ing. ing at 4 × 4 feet, as is done in Sikkim, alternate rows might be cut out at the end of the fourth year, leaving the trees standing at distances of 8 × 4 feet. Possibly the stools of the first cutting, standing in such deep shade as this close planting involves, would not send up coppice shoots, and it is scarcely desirable that they should do so. By a second cutting a year or two later, the distances might be increased to 8 × 8 feet. The stools formed from this and subsequent cuttings would probably coppice fairly well. Further cuttings of alternate rows or of alternate trees would follow, coppice shoots rising from each and being worked in the modes usual for coppice in Europe. It may also be found to answer to cut down entirely all the trees on a patch planted 4 × 4 feet as soon as they begin to impede each other's growth, which would in good soil be about the third or fourth year. The coppice on a patch so treated would grow freely, and so also would the weeds; cultivation would therefore be necessary. These methods are now being tried on the Sikkim plantation.

The rather discouraging results of coppicing, and the undoubted richness[2] in alkaloid of the bark covering the

Harvesting by uprooting the trees. larger roots of Cinchona trees, suggested to the resident manager of the Sikkim plantation (Mr. James A Gammie) that the plan of digging out the trees by their roots might be advantageous. Accordingly, during the past cold season about thirty-five acres of eight and nine-year old trees have been treated in this way. The operation of rooting out is not so formidable as might be expected. If a plantation is worked from below upwards, it is found that, after the lower row has been taken out, the trees are very easily eradicated by pulling them downwards, a little earth having been first removed from their roots at the upper side, and a rope being attached to the stem pretty far up, so as to give a long leverage. The collection of bark by the method of rooting out is estimated to cost $2\frac{1}{4}$ pies (·28 of a penny) per pound of green bark, as against $1\frac{3}{4}$ pies (·22 of a penny) by coppicing.

It seems not unlikely that uprooting might be conjoined with early coppicing. For example, a patch planted 4 × 4 feet might be thinned

---

[1] The increase in total outturn of bark per acre when close planting is adopted is very much greater than a superficial glance at the figures indicating the planting distances would lead one to suppose. Thus, while the adoption of a planting distance of 12 × 12 feet (as in the older parts of the Nilgiri plantations) gives 303 trees per acre, planting 6 × 6 feet gives 1,210 trees, and planting 4 × 4 feet (as in Sikkim) gives 2,722 trees per acre. This consideration is lost sight of in the calculations already quoted on the respective yields of mossing and coppicing on the Nilgiris. For a table of the number of plants to the acre according to planting distance see Appendix L.

[2] Mr. Wood's analyses shew that root bark contains about 8 per cent. of total alkaloids

to 8 × 8 at the end of the fourth year; and at the end of the eighth year the remaining trees might be uprooted. The ground in this method of uprooting is submitted to a thorough deep cultivation and may be replanted at once, or it may be allowed to lie fallow for some time before being replanted. The obvious objection to immediate replanting is, of course, that it is bad practice to replant with the same species; but, as nothing except the bark of the former crop will have been removed from the ground, this objection ought to go for little in the face of the immense advantage gained by a thorough upturning of the soil. Moreover, it is the custom on fir plantations in Scotland to replant with fir; and in the case of fir the old crop is almost entirely removed in the shape of timber. One advantage of replanting at once is that the expense of clearing the land is obviated, as in the process of uprooting it is cleaned to hand. By adopting a different planting distance from the last crop, the new plants could be made to occupy slightly different spots from their predecessors. If, however, it is deemed expedient to give the ground rest for a few years, a rotation on this basis could easily be established.

At certain seasons of the year the bark can be separated from the wood with great ease. This is the case in Sikkim during the greater part of the cold season, which, therefore, for this, as for other reasons, is the best for taking the bark crop. The barking is done by a gang of coolies, to whom the felled stem and branches are made over as fast as they are cut. Provided with a stout gardener's knife, a cooly in removing stem bark, or the bark of thick branches, first marks it off into long narrow slips by longitudinal and transverse incisions; he then separates one of the ends of a strip by putting his knife under it and pressing upwards; the end being freed, the remainder of the strip readily comes off. Bark from the smaller branches and twigs cannot of course be removed thus; but it is easily whittled off, care being taken to include as little wood in the whittlings as possible.

Removing the bark.

On being taken off the trees, the bark is laid to dry in rough sheds fitted up with open shelves made of split bamboo. These sheds are erected in any convenient place near the spot where the trees are being cut. When the bark has dried as far as is possible without artificial heat, it is carried off to the drying-house, a masonry building (near the factory) fitted up with shelving and supplied with arrangements for keeping charcoal fires lit. If the drying-house be kept well closed, the bark is speedily and thoroughly dried, and without being exposed to a temperature high enough to affect its chemical constitution.[1] When well dried, it can be stored without danger of deterioration.

Drying the bark.

---

[1] The temperature of the Sikkim drying-house ranges from 10° to 15° Fahr. above that of the open air.

CHAPTER VII.

ON THE LOCAL MANUFACTURE OF A CINCHONA FEBRIFUGE.

Commercial value of Red bark.

The Cinchona plantations on the Nilgiris yield practically two barks, Red bark and Crown. Red bark is rich in total alkaloids, but not very rich in Quinine, and the Quinine in it is difficult of extraction. This bark is of comparatively small value, therefore, to the Quinine-maker, although of great value to Government as a source of supply of a cheap febrifuge. Red bark is also of much value in Europe for decoctions (in other words it is a good druggist's bark), and recently large prices have been got for consignments bought by druggists. These rates are far beyond the value of the Quinines contained in such bark as estimated by a Quinine-maker. It is doubtful whether a European alkaloid-maker could, in fact, work Red bark for its alkaloids at their present price, and pay for the bark at the rates recently given in London for Nilgiri-grown produce. The present good prices should undoubtedly be taken advantage of by all planters to whom gain is the sole object. If, however, the profits of sale are to be taken advantage of, the idea of at once supplying a cheap febrifuge must be abandoned. The latter is the avowed object of Government, and no passing commercial advantage should be allowed to interfere with its realisation.

The following table, extracted from Mr. Broughton's report to the Government of Madras, dated 9th August 1873, gives analyses of certain Nilgiri barks which were sent to England for sale, and may be taken as a fair example of the produce of the Government plantations there :—

	Mossed Red Bark, Neddivuttum.	Renewed Red Bark, Neddivuttum.	Grey Bark.	Red Bark, Neddivuttum.	Red Bark, Pykara.	Branch Red Bark.	Crown Bark, Nodivuttum.	Crown Bark, Pykara.	Mossed Crown Bark, Dodabetta.	Crown Bark, Dodabetta.	Branch Crown Bark.
Total alkaloids	6·20	5·82*	2·75	4·45†	5·11	3·58	4·32‡	3·42§	6·60	3·61¶	0·91
Quinine and Quinicine	1·14	3·25	...	1·31	0·97	1·33	3·09	2·32	3·89	2·07	...
Cinchonidine and Cinchonine	5·06	2·57	2·75	3·14	4·14	2·25	1·24	1·10	2·71	1·54	...
Pure Sulphate of Quinine obtained crystallised	0·74	2·62	...	0·74	0·62	0·81	3·11	2·39	3·86	2·04	...
Pure Sulphate of Cinchonidine obtained crystallised	3·47	0·68	1·00	1·61	2·22	1·14	0·85	0·67	1·00	0·90	...

* Mean of three analyses.   ‡ Mean of two analyses.   ‖ Mean of two analyses.
† Mean of two analyses.   § Do. do.   ¶ Do. do.

Commercial value of Crown bark.

Crown bark is, on the other hand, rich in crystallisable Quinine, and is nearly as highly valued by the Quinine-maker as good American Yellow. If any bark is to be sent to England for sale, Crown Bark should be sent. The Red bark trees are, however, by far the most numerous on the Government and other plantations in India and the

Colonies. This species is hardier, grows better, and yields about a third more bark than the Pale or Crown bark. The utilisation of Red bark by manufacture in India is therefore of the highest importance.

The Sikkim plantations consist of Red and Yellow bark trees. Yel-
low bark, which has been a failure on the
The Sikkim barks are Nilgiris, promises to be a success there. In cha-
Red and Yellow. racter Yellow resembles Crown bark, but is even more esteemed by the Quinine-maker. It is hardly necessary to say that, both being easy to work, Crown and Yellow barks would be very much preferable to Red bark as sources for the manufacture in India of a cheap febrifuge if *officinalis* and *calisaya* trees could be got to grow as luxuriantly as *succirubra*.

As the result of his experiments, Mr. Broughton decided on issuing
as "the cheap febrifuge" wanted for India a
Mr. Broughton's Amor- preparation called Amorphous Quinine, which
phous Quinine. consists of the total alkaloids of Cinchona bark in the form of a non-crystalline powder, mixed to some extent with the resin and red-colouring matter so abundant in Red bark. This alkaloid was accepted by the medical faculty in the Madras Presidency as a remedy in malarious fever scarcely, if at all, inferior to Quinine. Mr. Broughton's own account of his mode of preparing this alkaloid, is given by himself as follows[1]:—

"6. The actual Cinchona bases being, of course, the active medicinal constituents
in the sulphates or other salts employed as febrifuge, it
Mr. Broughton's manufactur- was necessarily believed that the bases themselves would be
ing process described. as effective medicines as their salts. The considerable
Therapeutical considerations amount of tinctures and extracts of Cinchona bark still em-
and result. ployed in medicinal practice clearly shews the efficacy of salts other than sulphates, nor, as far as I could learn, do the preparations made from Cinchona bark destitute of real Quinine shew any failure in febrifuge efficacy, a fact readily explained by the results of the Madras Cinchona Commission. Pure Quinine Sulphate contains but 73·55 per cent. of Quinine. It was, therefore, believed that a preparation of the Cinchona alkaloids, in the proportion that they naturally exist in the barks, which would contain about ninety-seven per cent. of the pure bases, would admit of exactly the same medicinal doses being employed as of Quinine Sulphate. If there should be, for which there is no evidence, a somewhat inferior febrifuge quality in the alkaloids other than Quinine, this would, it was believed, be compensated for by the larger amount of the real bases in the preparation in comparison with Quinine Sulphate. The report of the Medical Inspector-General, attached to G. O. No. 29 of the 11th January 1871, appears subsequently to corroborate these suppositions, as he states it to be 'a remedy in malarious fever, scarcely, if at all, inferior to Quinine.'

* * * * * * *

"8. In a report appearing in Return on Cinchona Cultivation, 1870, page 243,
paragraph 54, and more fully in a Memoir in Phil
Alkaloids exist in bark as Trans. Roy. Soc., 1870, I shew that six-sevenths of the
insoluble Quino-tannates. alkaloids in the bark of *C. succirubra* occur in the form of Quino-tannates. As this salt is nearly insoluble in water, the presence of a strong acid is necessary for its decomposition and complete solution of the alkaloid. It is this circumstance which constitutes the main difficulty in the preparation of alkaloid, since, even after the tannates have been decomposed in hot or dilute solutions, they partially reform when the same solutions become cold or are increased in strength.

* * * * * * *

N. B.—The numbering of the paragraphs of Mr. Broughton's letter is retained in the above quotation.

[1] Mr. Broughton's letter to Secretary, Madras Government, dated 1st December 1873.

"14. The method I have adopted is quite similar in principle to the usual method that, since the time of Pelletier, has prevailed in manufactories of Cinchona alkaloids. It consists in precipitating the alkaloids in an insoluble state and subsequently separating them from the mass of impurities with which they are mixed by solution in alcohol. The method is, however, so contrived that the very cheapest materials are used, and the greatest economy is practicable with those materials which are not found on the plantations. The only material of which the consumption is large is that of wood fuel, which some years ago it was believed would be furnished in any amount by the Cinchona plantations by trees which had been coppiced. This, however, has not been the case, owing to the adoption of Mr. McIvor's system of mossing, respecting which I have already expressed an opinion which I need not further reiterate.

Principle of method in use.

"15. The process was first tried in my small laboratory at Ootacamund, and I found that from eighty to ninety-five per cent. of the total amount of alkaloid in the bark was obtained by it. If done with analytic precision, which, of course, cannot be practically carried out in a manufactory, 97·1 per cent. of that amount is obtainable, though I have never obtained this result when working with native coolies, but only when the work was performed by myself or by my laboratory assistant.

Experimental results of method.

"16. The first product of this process, named by the late Principle Medical Inspector-General "Amorphous Quinine," was prepared in the small experimental manufactory erected at Ootacamund, where enough was prepared from Red bark grown at Neddivuttum for a fair trial of its medical efficacy. The results of its medical trial are contained in a report of the Principal Medical Inspector-General attached to G. O. No. 29 of the 11th January 1871, which were considered highly favourable.

First trials of manufacture.

"17. I will now describe the method of manufacture I have adopted, which, though in the course of work it has been constantly modified and improved, is, of course, susceptible of further improvements in detail.

Description of method now employed. Extraction of bark.

The bark in long strips, exactly as taken from the tree, is placed in a copper pan with 1½ per cent. of sulphuric acid [1] and a quantity of water that has already been used for the fourth extraction of nearly spent bark, and is boiled for an hour. The liquid and bark are then separated by strong pressure in a screw press, the former falling in a wooden vat placed underneath. The squeezed and nearly dry bark is again boiled with liquid that has been used for a third boiling of other bark, and another half per cent. of acid is added. After an hour's boiling it is again squeezed. It is then again boiled with a liquid that has come off nearly-spent bark, again squeezed, and finally boiled with water. During these four boilings the bark after each squeezing diminishes greatly in bulk and becomes almost pulp, so that it occupies far less room in a pan at the third boiling than it did at the first. The order in which the several liquids used in extraction are employed depends on the qualities of bark under manufacture; but it is so arranged as to obtain finally a liquid containing as much alkaloid as possible in solution, and also that, as far as possible, the bark should be exhausted of alkaloid. Finally, there arrives a point when the amount of alkaloid in the bark has become so small as not to repay the expense of further extraction. The bark then is dried in the sun and used as fuel.

"18. The liquid, which, if the foregoing be judiciously managed, should be intensely bitter and strong, is evaporated to about one-sixth of its bulk, transferred to a tub, and allowed to cool. It is then decomposed by neutralisation with milk of lime, which precipitates the alkaloids, decomposing the Quino-tannates and Sulphates with formation of insoluble lime salts. A slight excess of lime is always added. After standing for a day, precipitate is separated by filtration, squeezed, dried, and powdered in a common ragi mill.[2] The liquid, which contains abundance of Calcic Quinate in solution, is thrown away.

Precipitation of extracts with lime.

"19. As first conducted, the evaporation mentioned in the foregoing paragraph was omitted, the precipitation being at once performed in the original liquid. But as alkaloid is unfortunately slightly soluble in lime-water, this proceeding was found

Evaporation was at first dispensed with. Necessity for the use of lime.

---

[1] This is the amount of acid employed for *trunk* bark; for *prunings* but one per cent. or even less is ordinarily used.

[2] The mill used by the peasantry for grinding their grain.

to produce considerable waste, and therefore it was found necessary to evaporate in order to reduce this waste to a minimum. In India lime must necessarily be the precipitant, as it is by far the cheapest of all the alkaline bases. I have tried both English Caustic Soda and Indian Soudoo as precipitants of the alkaloid, but for many reasons do not now employ them.

"20. The powdered lime precipitate is then packed in the apparatus, of which a drawing is given; ABCD being a large cone of sheet iron, through the centre of which passes an upright tube, the upper end of which terminates in a crosspiece with four openings. The lower end of the tube is also open, and supported on a flat perforated circular disc (CD) made of sheet iron. This allows it to rest in the cone. Below, and tightly fitting to the lower part of the cone, is an under copper vessel (FG). The cone is supported by chains, and above it is placed in connection with the lower end of a simple worm-tub (not shewn in the drawing) by means of a tube (H). The powdered lime precipitate is filled in the cone till immediately under the cross tube (E). The upper lid of the cone is fitted on and alcohol poured on till, by passing through the precipitate, the lower vessel becomes about a third full. The spirit is then saturated with alkaloid, which is neutralised with care by diluted sulphuric acid, of which the strength is known. Then the upper lid of the cone is put into connection with the upper condenser by the tube E, and a fire is lighted below. The spirit boiling in FG rises in vapour through the inner tube and passes out at the four openings of the cross-piece. It here generally condenses to a liquid, but if not it passes into the copper condenser, where it of course condenses. so that by a judicious arrangement of the fire a layer of liquid is kept on the surface of the precipitate. A gauge (BI) allows this to be seen from the outside. If the fire is, however, kept too fierce, no harm can ensue, since, if the layer of liquid rises in consequence higher than the percolation through the precipitate removes it, it simply passes down through the centre tube into the lower vessel. Hence the apparatus is self-acting, and the cooly work-people have no access to the alcohol, which is all inside the apparatus. A small amount of alcohol by constant circulation through the apparatus thus completely dissolves the whole of the Cinchona bases without any waste of spirit or alkaloid. Every two days the alkaloid is neutralised with dilute acid. If this be done with moderate care, there is no chance of the copper under-vessel being in the least attacked, but if very carelessly done, a mere trace of Oxide of Copper is dissolved. This, however, rarely occurs; but if it does, it is readily remedied subsequently.

Proceedings employed to exhauste with alcohol.

"21. The fire is thus kept up until the whole of the alkaloid is dissolved and passes into the lower vessel. This state of things is known by the alkalinity of the liquid in the lower vessel not increasing; but to make sure, the spirit dropping from the cone is usully tested when the process draws near its end. When finished, the exhausted precipitate does not contain a trace of alkaloid, all being in the lower vessel. The lower vessel is then removed and the alcohol separated by distillation. Water is also poured on the cone, in order to wash out the alcohol with which the precipitate is still moistened, until the latter is quite removed. The alcohol is thus nearly all recovered and is purified for another operation by distillation. With care, waste of spirit practically does not occur, but I have been unable yet to prevent all loss of spirit from the carelessness with which every operation in this country appears more or less attended. The loss, however, has not exceeded six per cent. and has fallen frequently much below this.

Recovery and actual waste of alcohol.

"22. The alkaloid sulphate in the lower vessel is suddenly diluted with about ten times its bulk of cold water. This separates a considerable amount of black resin. Since the contamination of copper occurred in Bengal in the alkaloid, I have always as a precaution added a small amount of a dilute acidulated solution of Sodic Sulphide to the liquid. This completely removes copper if it be present, though with very moderate care it is completely unnecessary. The solution is still, however, coloured with impurities, to remove which a small amount of alkaloid is precipitated by the addition of dilute Caustic Soda, which carries down with it the colouring matters. The whole is then filtered through a cloth bag, and the alkaloid in the filtrate is precipitated by Caustic Soda, separated by filtration, squeezed, dried, and powdered. It is then 'Amorphous Quinine.' Before it leaves the manufactory, as a precautionary measure, it is always tested for copper.

Purification and precipitation of alkaloid.

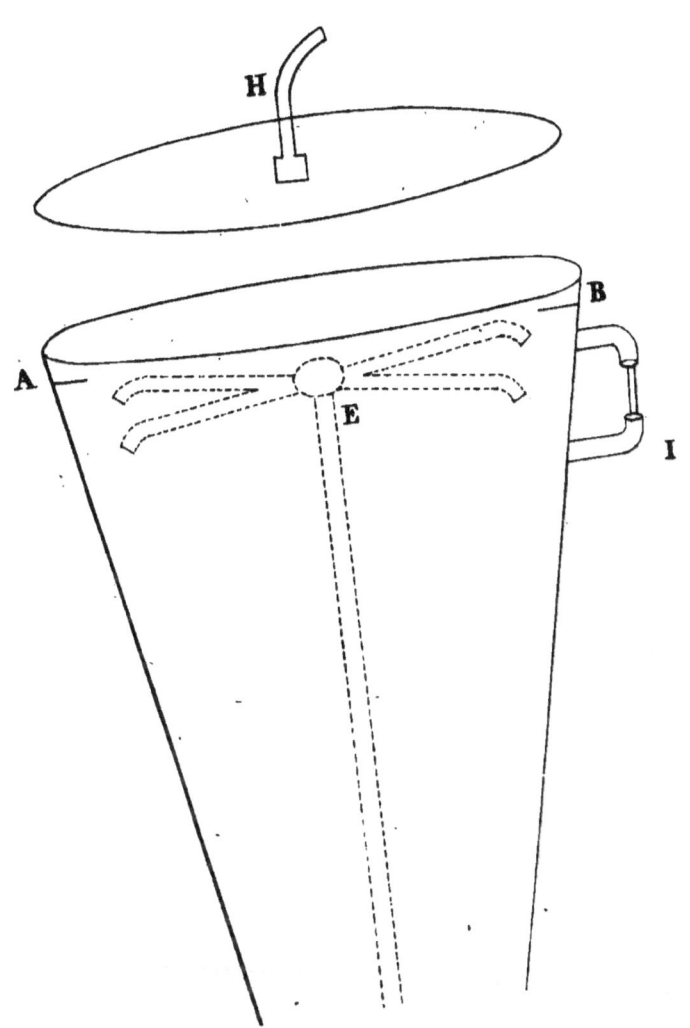

ON THE LOCAL MANUFACTURE OF A CINCHONA FEBRIFUGE. 73

"23. Formerly, from the ashes of the fuel employed, Caustic Potash was prepared, to use as precipitant, instead of soda. But lately, so small an amount of potash has occurred in the ashes, that this has been discontinued. If the Cinchona wood from coppiced trees was employed as fuel, this might be again resumed, and thus a further saving effected.

Potash should be obtained from ashes of fuel.

"24. Sulphuric acid has been used in preference to hydrochloric acid, mainly because it is the cheaper acid. While the cost is nearly the same, the effective work produced by the sulphuric acid is nearly double that of hydrochloric acid for equal weights. It has also some better qualities for transit through the tropics. The use of sulphuric acid has also some chemical advantages which I need not further particularise. With Red bark there is, unfortunately, no fear of the sudden crystallisation of Quinine Sulphate on the dilution mentioned in paragraph 22, as there would be with Crown bark.

Why sulphuric acid is preferred for extraction of bark.

"25. The alkaloid which is carried down in connection with the precipitated resin, and in the purification by fractional precipitation, is, of course, from time to time obtained free from impurities by the obvious methods of drying and digestion with dilute acids, &c. Thus obtained, it is generally very pure and colourless.

Alkaloid contained in the resin is not wasted.

"26. Throughout the whole course of manufacture, simplicity of arrangement has been carried out as far as possible. The reasons for this are—

Simple apparatus throughout has been preferred.

1st.—That certain labour-saving appliances which are used in England would here be a source of considerable expense, and are obtainable with great difficulty and delay. Until alkaloid manufacture in South India has proved itself a permanent success, I have therefore felt it wiser to refrain from all dispensable expenditure for apparatus for which simple substitutes could be provided.

2nd.—That the simpler the apparatus, the more readily are they repaired, when necessary, in India.

3rd.—The intelligence of Canarese coolies on the Nilgiris is fully exercised by the simplest proceedings of manufacture; therefore any increase in their apparent complexity has to be made with a risk of loss and injury to the apparatus.

* * * * * * *

"35. I will indicate the sources of the loss of alkaloid which occur in the manufacture, nearly the whole of which are preventible only at a greatly increased cost of labour and product:—

Sources of waste of alkaloid in manufacture.

"*1st.*—The not quite complete exhaustion of the bark of alkaloid on first extraction with acidulated water. Usually the bark at the end of the boilings described in paragraph 16 of this report still contains a small amount of alkaloid, which another boiling and squeezing would remove. This is not now performed, as the small amount of alkaloid obtained would not repay the cost of the labour, fuel, and subsequent evaporation.

"*2nd.*—Spilling and waste of extract, and occasionally of bark itself, by the carelessness and indifference of the coolies. This is not preventible in India.

"*3rd.*—Waste of material in grinding the lime precipitate, and in final powdering of the alkaloid. This may, with care and training, be diminished, but cannot entirely be obviated.

"*4th.*—The solubility to a small extent of the alkaloid in lime-water. At the beginning of the year 1872-73 loss from this source occurred. It has since, as I have before mentioned, been prevented by the evaporation of the liquid extract of bark down to a small bulk, before the precipitation with milk of lime is performed. I cannot fairly estimate the amount of waste that has occurred from this source, but believe it will not have exceeded 20 lbs. of alkaloid.

"36. As a measure of precaution, I have repeatedly tested whether the lime precipitate is completely exhausted of alkaloid by the alcohol before throwing it away, and have always found that no alkaloid is wasted by imperfect exhaustion, as might otherwise be naturally supposed."

74 CINCHONA CULTIVATION IN INDIA.

Up to the end of the financial year 1872-73, about six hundred pounds of Amorphous Cinchona alkaloids had been produced at the Nilgiri factory. It was found, however, that, after calculating at its manufacturing value [1] the price of the bark used, Mr. Broughton's product cost more than ordinary commercial Quinine. The factory has accordingly been closed, and arrangements are to be made for the disposal of the whole of the Nilgiri bark otherwise than by local manufacture.

Results of local manufacture in the Nilgiris.

The Sikkim plantations are younger than those on the Nilgiris. No Quinologist was appointed to them until the end of the year 1873, when Mr. C. H. Wood was sent out by the Secretary of State. Owing to delays in the arrival of his laboratory apparatus, Mr. Wood was unable to begin work before March 1874. Some time was necessarily spent in the preliminary work of analysing the various barks produced in the plantation, with the view of determining the influence of elevation, manure, &c., on them, and also in conducting experiments with the object of settling on the most advantageous mode of manufacturing an efficient febrifuge. Actual manufacturing operations did not therefore begin until 1875.

Local manufacture in Sikkim.

The method at present in operation in the factory in Sikkim is simple in the extreme. Its principle has been thus described:—

Sikkim method of manufacture.

"In this method," writes Mr. Wood,[2] "the bark (roughly powdered) is first exhausted with cold acidulated water, and the resulting liquor precipitated by a caustic alkali. It is therefore essentially the same as that advocated by Dr. DeVry, although I have found it desirable to modify the plan of precipitation he recommended." . . . . "No fuel is required except what may be necessary to dry the alkaloid obtained. No expensive machinery is involved, the only plant required being some wooden tubs and calico filters. Skilled labour is unnecessary, and very little supervision is wanted."

The following detailed account of the process has been given by Mr. Wood:—

"*General object of the process.*—The present method of treating Cinchona bark was adopted as a temporary measure to afford the means of ascertaining the medicinal value of the proposed febrifuge. It was considered undesirable to incur any expenditure for factory buildings, machinery, or skilled labour, until the efficacy of the product as a remedial agent had been thoroughly determined by extensive trials. Consequently, it was necessary to so arrange the process that it could be conducted for some time on a considerable scale, and involve no other appliances than such as were already at hand.

"*General nature of the process.*—The dry bark is crushed into small pieces (but not powdered) and is put into wooden casks, where it is macerated in the cold with very dilute hydrochloric acid. The liquor is then run off into wooden vessels and mixed with an excess of a strong solution of caustic soda; a precipitate forms, which is collected on calico filters, and well washed with water. The precipitate is then dried at a gentle heat and powdered. It constitutes the crude febrifuge, which is next submitted to a process of purification. In the latter process a certain weight of the crude product is dissolved in dilute sulphuric acid, and a small quantity of a solution of sulphur in caustic soda is added to the liquor. After the lapse of 24 hours the liquor is carefully filtered. The filtrate is mixed with caustic soda, and the resulting precipitate collected on calico, washed with a small quantity of water, dried and powdered; it is then ready for issue, and is sent out under the name of 'Cinchona febrifuge.'

---

[1] The prices taken by the Commission appointed to enquire into the working of the factory are—Dry trunk bark 2s, and branch bark 6d., a pound.

[2] Report of Government Quinologist, British Sikkim, dated 5th August 1874.

ON THE LOCAL MANUFACTURE OF A CINCHONA FEBRIFUGE. 75

"*Arrangement of the factory sheds.*—A position was chosen conveniently near the dry bark godowns, and so situated on the side of the hill that a copious supply of water could be obtained at a level with the roof of the sheds in which the maceration is conducted.

"These sheds are rough temporary erections, constructed with saplings and a mat or thatch roof. Down the centre an open drain is cut to carry off the waste liquor. Over this drain some wooden stands are placed, on which the calico filters rest. The filters are formed by tying a square piece of calico to a wooden frame by the four corners. On each side of the shed is placed a row of 21 casks, standing on end upon a stand which elevates them about 2 feet from the ground. They are empty beer barrels, which have been purchased from the Commissariat Department at Darjeeling, the head removed, and the cask thoroughly cleansed; a hole is cut in the side of the cask at a level with the bottom, and closed with a cork. In front of the casks a row of tubs, formed by cutting beer barrels in halves, is placed, so that on uncorking the barrels the liquor will run out into the tubs.

"Outside the shed, at one end, are a couple of large wooden vats at such an elevation that liquid can flow from them along a bamboo trough into any one of the barrels in the shed. The capacity of the vats, up to a mark on the inside near the top, is accurately determined. Water is run into the vat up to the mark, and a certain quantity of muriatic acid is added, and the whole well mixed. This diluted acid can then be run into any one of the casks in a line with the vat by means of a bamboo trough. In addition to the macerating sheds, there is a small brick building, heated with charcoal, in which the precipitate is dried; also a separate shed in which the process of purification is conducted.

"*Method of conducting the process.*—The casks are worked in sets of three, and are marked A, B, C.

"In each shed there are 14 sets, 7 on each side. Each cask receives one maund of dry bark, which undergoes four successive macerations, the liquor being moved in rotation through the three casks. Each maceration lasts half a week. The liquor used for the fourth and last maceration is acidulated water drawn from the vat. When this is run off, it is moved into the next cask to form the third liquor. When this is drawn off, it forms the second liquor for another cask, and, when transferred from that, it goes on to new bark, from which it is drawn off and precipitated. The following table will shew the manner in which this rotation is effected. Of course in starting a new shed every cask contains dry bark, consequently the system of rotation is not brought into full operation until after the first fortnight; and it is only after the shed has been in operation for 3½ weeks (June 7 in table) that the liquor for precipitation has been used for four macerations. The table is drawn for a new shed; after June 7th, it is in regular order.

"The liquor that is for precipitation is run into the tubs. The other liquors are drawn into wooden buckets and poured into the proper casks. The new acid is then drawn from the vats. The diluted acid is made in the vat by adding 1 gallon of muriatic acid to every 100 gallons of water (10 fluid ounces to each cubic foot).

"If three sheds are employed, No. 1 is worked on Mondays and Thursdays, No. 2 on Tuesdays and Fridays, and No. 3 on Wednesdays and Saturdays. It will be seen by the table that each set of three casks exhausts one maund of dry bark per week. Three sheds, therefore, containing 42 casks each, would exhaust 42 maunds of bark every week.

"The weight of acid used in the exhaustion is 6⅓ per cent. of the weight of dry bark. It is obtained from Mr. Waldie's chemical works, at a cost of 3¼ annas per pound in Calcutta.

"To precipitate the saturated liquor, a solution of caustic soda is added in excess. The caustic soda is obtained from England in 5-cwt. drums, costing from £15 to £20 per ton in London. One part of this is dissolved in three parts of water, and the solution stored in iron vessels. The quantity to be added to the bark liquor must be judged of by the appearance produced. When a sufficient quantity has been introduced, the precipitate assumes a somewhat curdy condition.

"About 6½ pounds of solid soda are used for every 100 pounds of dry bark.

"The filtration is not commenced until the following day, when the liquor is transferred to the calico strainers which have been well wetted. The first portions that run through are returned until the liquid passes of a bright ruby colour; it is then allowed to flow away by the drain. After all the liquor has drained off, water is passed through the precipitate until it ceases to acquire a red tint. The alkaloids on the filter should then be of a uniform cream colour. The precipitate is now dried and reduced to a fine powder, which is stored in suitable bins. It constitutes the crude febrifuge.

"*The process of purification.*—The precipitate during the act of drying acquires a slightly reddish-brown colour. It is therefore submitted to a process of purification. Fourteen gallons of water are mixed with two pints of sulphuric acid, and twenty pounds of the dry powder are introduced. The alkaloids dissolve, and a quantity of colouring matter remains insoluble. About half a pint of a solution of sulphur in caustic soda is now stirred in, and the whole allowed to stand for twenty-four hours. It is then filtered through calico into a clean vessel, care being taken to get the liquor perfectly bright. About 6 gallons of water are used to wash the sediment left on the filters. The clear filtrate is thoroughly mixed with solution of soda to precipitate the alkaloids; the precipitate is collected on calico, washed with a small quantity of water, drained, dried, and reduced to fine powder; it is then ready for issue.

"Wooden tubs are used for this process, but they are not so well suited for the purpose as enamelled iron or earthenware. The purification is conducted in a separate shed by a man who is confined to that work.

"*The labour employed.*—The only workmen employed in the factory are Nepalese coolies. When the process is once brought into full operation, it is found that these men readily master every detail, and conduct the whole thing with all the care and accuracy that is required. But of course the factory is under the supervision of Mr. Gammie, the officer in charge of the plantations, who visits it once a day, and sees that the work is being properly performed.

"*The bark used.*—Dry *succirubra* bark only is employed. Moreover, care is taken to mix the root, stem, and branch bark together in as nearly as possible the proportions in which they are yielded by the plantations. This mixture is broken into small pieces, and a maund of it goes into each cask. This is done to insure uniformity of composition in the product. Green bark is never operated on. It will be seen that the arrangement of the process requires that a certain weight of bark should be put into the casks every week throughout the year. This could not be done with green bark, because bark is only taken from the trees twice per annum. Apart from this, however, it has been found that dry bark yields a much better product, and quite as large a quantity. The small cost of drying the bark is more than counterbalanced by the advantages gained.

"*Temporary object of the process.*—It must be remembered that this method has only been adopted to furnish a large supply of febrifuge for trial; it does not profess to make the most economical use possible of the bark. The factory is estimated to turn out during the present financial year 4,800 pounds of febrifuge, which, at a rupee an ounce, will pay the whole cost of the plantations and manufacture for the year. If the product proves to be of permanent value as a remedial agent, it is probable that the process will be considerably modified to produce greater economy, but involving the use of permanent buildings and machinery.

SCHED No. 1.

Casks marked A, B, C.

Thursday, May 13th	Put dilute acid in A	1st liquor for A. (New bark is in A.)
Monday, „ 17th	Run liquor from A and precipitate. Put dilute acid in A	2nd liquor for A.
Thursday, „ 20th	Move liquor from A to B . . Put dilute acid in A	1st liquor for B. (New bark is in B.) 3rd for A.
Monday, „ 24th	Run liquor off B and precipitate. Move liquor from A to B . . . Put dilute acid on A	2nd liquor for B. 4th for A.

SCHED No. 1 (*continued*).

Day		Operations	Status
Thursday, „ 27th		Move liquor from B to C Move liquor from A to B Clean out A.	1st liquor for C. (New bark is in C.) 3rd for B.
Monday, „ 31st		Run liquor off C and precipitate. Move liquor from B to C Put dilute acid on B	2nd liquor for C. 4th for B.
Thursday, June 3rd		Move liquor from C to A Move liquor from B to C Clean out B.	1st liquor for A. (New barks is in A.) 3rd for C.
Monday, „ 7th		Run liquor off A and precipitate. Move liquor from C to A Put dilute acid on C	2nd liquor for A. 4th for C.
Thursday, „ 10th		Move liquor from A to B Move liquor from C to A Clean out C.	1st liquor for B. (New bark in in B.) 3rd for A.
Monday, „ 14th		Run liquor off B and precipitate. Move liquor from A to B Put dilute acid on A	2nd liquor for B. 4th for A.
Thursday, „ 17th		Move liquor from B to C Move liquor from A to B Clean out A.	1st liquor for C. (New bark is in C.) 3rd for B.
Monday, „ 21st		Run liquor off C and precipitate. Move liquor from B to C Put dilute acid on B	2nd liquor for C. 4th for B.
Thursday, „ 24th		Move liquor from C to A Move liquor from B to C Clean out B.	1st liquor for A. (New bark is in A.) 3rd for C.

After making a very moderate estimate as to the actual number of trees on the plantation and of the outturn of bark per tree (*viz.*, one and a half pounds in 8 years), and after covering every expense and including interest at four per cent. on all the capital sunk in the Government Cinchona enterprise in Sikkim, Mr. Wood calculates that there can soon be yielded by this rough process from 130,000 to 140,000 ounces (or from 3¾ to 4 tons) annually of an efficient febrifuge at a cost of rather less than one rupee per ounce. But more complete methods of extraction are now under trial by Mr. Wood, which give promise of a still cheaper rate for the outturn. Taken in large bulk the Sikkim Red Bark yields a mixed alkaloid of an almost uniform composition, which Mr. Wood gives as follows:—

Crystallisable Quinine	15·5 parts.
Amorphous Quinine	17·0 „
Cinchonine	33·5 „
Cinchonidine	29·0 „
Colouring matter, &c.	5·0 „
Total	100·0

An approximate[1] idea of the commercial value of this compound may be got by calculating what it would cost to make up a compound of similar proportions of the sulphates of the cinchona alkaloids as sold in the London market. The prices of these sulphates fluctuate greatly, and those of the alkaloids other than Quinine do so more especially. And, although at the present time plentiful, there is no guarantee that these alkaloids could always be had in any quantity, even at a considerably enhanced price. As has already been explained, they are by-products of the manufacture of Quinine and do not exist in large proportion in the barks used by Quinine manufacturers. They exist largely in Red bark, which is at present chiefly a druggist's and not a Quinine-maker's bark, and were a Quinine-maker obliged to resort to Red bark he probably could not afford to pay current rates for it and to sell its alkaloids also at current rates. The Sikkim alkaloid at one rupee an ounce will in all probability remain very much cheaper than a similar mixture purchased in Europe, and it will have the great advantage of being always available at one price. The establishment of the therapeutic value of the alkaloids other than Quinine has, however, been really one of the results of the Government Cinchona enterprise : there is therefore nothing unfair in regarding 130,000 ounces of the Sikkim product as nearly equal in money value (as it apparently is in therapeutic efficiency) to a similar amount of Quinine which, at nine shillings an ounce, it would cost the State £58,500 sterling to purchase in London.

Therapeutic value of the Sikkim Cinchona febrifuge. The Sikkim alkaloid has already been submitted to a careful trial by physicians attached to the four leading hospitals in Calcutta : it has also been tried in the Burdwan fever. The reports[2] of the gentlemen who tried the preparation are so favourable that Dr. Cockburn, the Deputy Surgeon-General of the Presidency Circle, has given it as his opinion that there is "sufficient evidence to shew that the drug may be brought into general use." Larger quantities are now being issued for trial in other parts of India. Should this drug be accepted by the medical profession in India as an efficient febrifuge, they will be provided with a means of combating the commonest disease in the country such as they never before possessed. It is notorious that its high price has prevented and still prevents the sufficiently free use of Quinine in dispensary and other practice among the poor, and, until a cheaper substitute be given to the medical profession and to the general public, the old and ineffectual combat with malarious fever is likely to continue. With a good febrifuge at a rupee or twelve annas an ounce, malarious fever should be robbed of three-fourths of its annual victims, and the poor of this land be thus attached to their paternal Government by yet another bond.

---

[1] Only approximate, because, [whereas the Sikkim product consists of the pure uncombined alkaloids, the commercial sulphates consist of a comparatively costly alkaloid chemically combined with a considerable percentage of sulphuric acid, which is one of the cheapest of chemicals.

[2] Extracts from these reports will be found in Appendix M.

APPENDICES.

APPENDIX A.

List of the chief Modern Works relating to Cinchona (from Flückiger and Hanbury's Pharmacographia, page 328.)

Berg (Otto), *Cinarinden der pharmakognostischen Sammlung zu Berlin.* Berlin, 1866, 4to, 148 pages, and 10 plates shewing the microscopic structure of barks.

Bergen (Heinrich voh), *Monographie der China.* Hamburg, 1826, 4to, 348 pages, and 7 coloured plates representing the following barks :—China rubra, Huanuco, Calisaya, flava, Huamalies, Loxa, Jaen. An exhaustive work for its period in every direction.

Blue-books—*East India (Cinchona Plant),* folio.—

A.—Copy of correspondence relating to the introduction of the Cinchona plant into India, and to proceedings connected with its cultivation, from March 1852 to March 1863.
Ordered by the House of Commons to be printed, 20th March 1863. 272 pages.
Contains correspondence of Royle, Markham, Spruce, Pritchett, Cross, McIvor, Anderson and others, illustrated by 5 maps.

B.—Copy of further correspondence relating to the introduction of the Cinchona plant into India, and to proceedings connected with its cultivation, from April 1863 to April 1866.
Ordered by the House of Commons to be printed, 18th June 1866. 379 pages.
Contains monthly reports of the plantations on the Nilgiri Hills; annual reports for 1863-64 and 1864-65, with details of method of propagation and cultivation, barking, mossing, attacks of insects, illustrated by woodcuts and 4 plates; report of Cross's journey to Pitayo, with map: Cinchona cultivation in Wynaad, Coorg, the Pulney Hills and Travancore, with map: in British Sikkim, the Kangra Valley (Punjab), the Bombay Presidency, and Ceylon.

C.—Copy of all correspondence between the Secretary of State for India and the Governor-General, and the Governors of Madras and Bombay, relating to the cultivation of Cinchona plants from April 1866 to April 1870.
Ordered by the House of Commons to be printed, 9th August 1870.
Contains reports on the Nilgiri and other plantations, with map: appointment of Mr. Broughton as analytical chemist, his reports and analyses; reports on the relative efficacy of the several Cinchona alkaloids; on Cinchona cultivation at Darjeeling and in British Burma.

Delondre (Augustin Pierre) et Bouchardat (Apollinaire), *Quinologie.* Paris, 1854, 4to, 48 pages, and 23 good coloured plates exhibiting all the barks then met with in commerce.

Gorkom (K. W. van), *Die Chinacultur auf Java,* Leipzig, 1869, 61 pages. An account of the management of the Dutch plantations.

Howard (John Eliot), *Illustrations of the Nueva Quinologia of Pavon.* London, 1862, folio, 163 pages and 30 beautiful coloured plates. Figures of Cinchona, mostly taken from Pavon's specimens in the Herbarium of Madrid, and three plates representing the structure of several barks.

Howard (John Eliot), *Quinology of the East Indian Plantations.* London, 1869, fol. x. and 43 pages, with 3 coloured plates, exhibiting structural peculiarities of the barks of cultivated Cinchona.

Karsten (Hermann), *Die Medicinischen chinarinden Neu-Granada's*. Berlin, 1858, 8vo., 71 pages, and two plates shewing microscopic structure of a few barks. An English translation, prepared under the supervision of Mr. Markham, has been printed by the India Office, under the title of *Notes on the Medicinal Cinchona Barks of New Granada* by H. Karsten, 1861. The plates have not been reproduced.

Karsten (Hermann), *Floræ Columbiæ terrarumque adjacentium specimina selecta*. Berolini, 1858, folio. Beautiful coloured figures of various plants, including Cinchona, under which name are several species usually referred to other genera. Only the first three parts have been published.

Markham (Clements Robert). *The Cinchona species of New Granada, containing the botanical descriptions of the species examined by Drs. Mutis and Karsten; with some account of those botanists and of the results of their labours*. London, 1867, 8vo., 139 pages and 5 plates. The plates are not coloured, yet are good reduced copies of those contained in Karsten's *Floræ Columbiæ*; they represent the following: *Cinchona corymbosa, C. Trianæ, C. lancifolia, C. cordifolia, C. Tucujensis*.

Miquel (Friedrich Anton Wilhelm), *De Cinchonæ speciebus quibusdam, adjectis iis quæ in Javá coluntur. Commentatio ex Annalibus Musei Botanici Lugduno-Batavi exscripta*. Amstelodami, 1869, 4to, 20 pages.

Phœbus (Philipp), *Die Delondre-Bouchardat' schen China-Rinden*. Giessen, 1864, 8vo., 75 pages and a table. The author gives a description, without figures, of the microscopic structure of the type specimens figured iu Delondre and Bouchardat's *Quinologie*.

Planchon (Gustave), *Des Quinquinas*. Paris et Montpellier, 1864, 8vo., 150 pages. A description of the Cinchonas and their barks. An English translation has been issued under the superintendence of Mr. Markham by the India Office, under the title of *Peruvian Barks*, by Gustave Planchen, London, printed by Eyre and Spottiswoode, 1866.

Soubeiran (J. Leon) et Delondre (Augustin), *De l'introduction et de l'acclimation des Cinchonas dans les Indes néerlandaises et duns les Indes britanniques*. Paris, 1868, 8vo., 165 pages.

Triana (José), *Nouvelles études sur les Quinquinas*. Paris, 1870, folio, 80 pages and 33 plates. An interesting account of the labours of Mutis, illustrated by uncoloured copies of some of the drawings prepared by him in illustration of his unpublished *Quinologia de Bogotá*, especially of the several varieties of *Cinchona lancifolia*; also an enumeration and short descriptions of all the species of *Cinchona*, and of new Granadian plants (chiefly *Cascarilla*) formerly placed in that genus.

Vogl (August), *Chinarinden des Wiener Grosshandels und der Wiener Sammlungen*. Wien, 1867, 8vo, 134 pages, no figures. A very exhaustive description of the microscopic structure of the barks occurring in the Vienna market, or preserved in the museums of that city.

Weddell (Hugh Algernon), *Histoire naturelle des Quinquinas, ou monographie du genre Cinchona, suivie d'une description du genre Cascarilla et de quelques autres plantes de la méme tribu*. Paris, 1849, folio, 108 pages, 33 plates and map. Excellent uncoloured figures of Cinchona and some allied genera, and beautiful coloured drawings of the officinal barks. Plate I exhibits the anatomical structure of the plant; Plate II that of the bark.

Weddell (Hugh Algernon), *Notes sur les Quinquinas, extrait des Annales des Sciences naturelles*, 5éme série, tomes XI et XII, Paris, 1870, 8vo, 75 pages. A systematic arrangement of the genus *Cinchona*, and description of its (33) species, accompanied by useful remarks on their barks. An English translation has been printed by the India Office with the title, *Notes on the Quinquinas by H. A. Weddell*, London, 1871, 8vo, 64 pages. A German edition by Dr. F. A. Flückiger has also appeared under the title *Uebersicht der Cinchonen von H. A. Weddell*, Schaffhausen and Berlin, 1871, 8vo, 43 pages, with additions and indices.

APPENDIX B.

Statement shewing quantities of Quinæ Sulphas, Cinchonine, Cinchonidine, and Quinidine Sulphates, supplied to the Government Medical Depôts in India from 1867 to 1873, and price of the same.

BENGAL.	Quantity.	Price.
1867.	lbs.	£ s. d.
Quinæ Sulphas	1,083	0 4 0 per oz.
1868.		
Quium Sulphas	500	0 3 11 per oz.
„ „	1,617	3 10 8 per lb.
1869.		
Cinchonine, Sulphate of—	150	0 12 0 per lb.
Cinchonidine „	150	2 8 0 „
Quinidine „	150	2 8 0 „
Quinæ Sulphas	1,000	4 4 0 „
„ „ . . . . . · .	1,068	4 3 6 „
Cinchonine, Sulphate of—	350	0 9 6 „ .
Cinchonidine „	350	2 10 0 „
Quinidine „	350	2 10 0 ·„
1870.		
Quinæ Sulphas	1,160	4 19 8 per lb.
„ „	1,200	5 3 4 „
„ „	1,100	4 2 9 „
1871.		
Quinæ Sulphas . . . { lbs. 850 / „ 846 }	1,696	{ 5 5 10 per lb. and / 5 5 2 „ }
Cinchonidine Sulphate . . .	220	2 0 0 „
Quinidine . ·	160	2 14 0 „
1872.		
Quinæ Sulphas	500	6 0 0 per lb.
„ „	500	5 10 2 „
	760	4 18 8 „
Quinine, Neutral Sulphate of—	60	4 6 0 „
Quinæ Sulphas	950	4 18 8 „
Quinine, Neutral Sulphate of—	40	4 6 0 „
1873.	lbs. oz.	
Quinæ Sulphas	60 10	0 7 10 per oz.
„ „	2,546	0 16 0 per lb.

APPENDIX B—(continued).

	Quantity.	Price.
1874.	lbs.	
Quinæ Sulphas	5,524	
Cinchonidine, Sulphate of—	115	
Cinchonine ,,	86	
Quinidine ,,	302	
Cinchona Febrifuge, Darjeeling	20	
1875.		
Quinæ Sulphas	3,037	
Cinchonidine, Sulphate of—	116	
Cinchonine ,,	28	
Quinidine ,,	142	
Cinchona Febrifuge, Darjeeling	305	
Madras.		
1867.		
Quinæ Sulphas	200	0 4 3 per oz.
,, ,,	67	0 4 0 ,,
,, ,,	461	0 4 0 ,,
1868.		
Quinidine, Sulphate of—	133	0 5 0 per oz.
Cinchonidine, Sulphate of—	133	0 5 0 ,,
Cinchonine ,,	133	0 1 6 ,,
Quinæ Sulphas	645	3 18 8 per lb.
1869.		
Quinæ Sulphas	150	4 4 0 per lb.
Quinidine, Sulphate of—	150	2 4 0 ,,
Cinchonine ,,	61	0 10 0 ,,
Quinæ Sulphas	200	4 10 8 ,,
1870.		
Quinæ Sulphas	130	5 6 8 per lb.
Cinchonine, Sulphate of—	149	0 12 0 ,,
Cinchonidine ,,	208	2 0 0 ,,
Quinidine ,,	195	2 8 0 ,,
1871.		
Quinæ Sulphas	360	5 6 6 per lb.
Cinchonine, Sulphate of—	20	1 0 6 ,,
Quinæ Sulphas, bleached	15	0 8 3 per oz.
,, ,, unbleached	25	0 7 3 ,,
1872-73.	Lbs. oz.	
Quinæ Sulphas	300	5 0 0 per lb.
,, ,,	183 6	6 16 0 ,,
Cinchonine, Sulphate of—	48 8	
Cinchonidine ,,	10 9	
Quinidine ,,	71 14	

APPENDIX B—(concluded).

	Quantity.	Price.
1874.	lbs.	
Quinæ Sulphas	399	
Cinchonine, Sulphate of—	74	
Cinchonidine ,,	55	
Quinidine ,,	63	
1875.		
Quinæ Sulphas	632	
Cinchonine, Sulphate of—	124	
Cinchonidine ,,	68	
Quinidine ,,	124	
BOMBAY.		
1867.		
Quinæ Sulphas	500	0 4 2 per oz.
,, ,,	200	0 4 6 ,,
1868.		
Quinæ Sulphas	760	4 1 4 per lb
1869.		
Quinæ Sulphas	750	4 3 0 per lb.
1870.		
Quinæ Sulphas	700	4 17 6 per lb.
,, ,,	810	4 13 9 ,,
1871.		
Cinchonine	3	1 4 0 per lb.
Quinæ Sulphas	400	5 18 6 ,,
1872.		
Quinæ Sulphas	722	5 12 0 per lb.
1874.		
Quinæ Sulphas	1,000	
Cinchonidine, Sulphate of—	167	
Cinchonine ,,	...	
Quinidine ,,	...	
1875.		
Quinæ Sulphas	891	
Cinchonidine, Sulphate of—	345	
Cinchonine ,,	...	
Quinidine ,,	...	

APPENDIX C.

Cinchona plants permanently planted out, dates of planting, and number of acres by base and surface measurement under cultivation on the Government plantations on the Nilgiris.

Date	Total Number Species of Cinchona Plants planted.							Denison, Kilgarton, and Napier Estates, Neddivuttum.						
	Crown Barks.	Red Barks.	Yellow Barks.	Grey Barks.	Other Species.	Total.	Acres.	Crown Barks.	Red Barks.	Yellow Barks.	Grey Barks.	Other Species.	Acres, Surface.	Acres, Base.
1862-63	18,550	12,500	500	3,100	350	35,000	63	4,200	12,000	500	3,000	300	.....	.....
1863-64	20,432	7,700	1,000	2,500	.....	31,632	55	16,000	4,700	1,000	1,500	.....	.....	.....
1864-65	55,700	38,500	.....	3,519	.....	98,719	99	10,000	23,500	.....	2,500	.....	.....	.....
1865-66	45,500	34,030	.....	.....	.....	79,530	80	2,000	22,720	.....	.....	.....	.....	.....
1866-67	67,000	77,000	9,200	3,140	.....	156,340	156	5,000	49,000	8,000	1,140	.....	.....	.....
1867-68	150,701	163,800	9,600	14,000	1,600	339,701	340	15,000	94,800	6,200	9,000	.....	.....	.....
1868-69	65,000	77,945	7,700	2,500	.....	153,145	153	20,000	72,000	7,700	2,500	.....	.....	.....
1869-70	84,995	168,473	.....	.....	899	254,367	254	3,550	70,650	.....	.....	.....	.....	.....
1870-71	.....	.....	3,500	.....	.....	3,500	2	.....	.....	3,500	.....	.....	.....	.....
1871-72	700	.....	2,750	.....	800	4,250	5	.....	.....	2,750	.....	.....	.....	.....
1872-73	5,961	.....	.....	.....	7,994	13,955	16	.....	.....	.....	.....	.....	.....	.....
1873-74	15,743	.....	.....	.....	4,686	20,429	23	.....	.....	.....	.....	.....	.....	.....
Total	531,282	579,938	34,250	28,759	16,229	1,190,458	1,244	75,750	349,400	29,650	19,640	300	455	371·24

APPENDIX C—(continued).

Cinchona plants permanently planted out, dates of planting, and number of acres by base and surface measurement under cultivation on the Government plantations on the Nilgiris—(continued).

Date.	Dodabetta.							Wood and Hooker Estates, Pykara.						Stanley Estate, Mailcoondah.				
	Crown Barks.	Red Barks.	Yellow Barks.	Grey Barks.	Other Species.	Acres, Surface.	Acres, Base.	Crown Barks.	Red Barks.	Grey Barks.	Other Species.	Acres, Surface.	Acres, Base.	Crown Barks.	Red Barks.	Other Species.	Acres, Surface.	Acres, Base.
1862-63	14,350	500	.....	100	50	.....	.....	.....	.....	.....	.....	.....	.....	.....	.....	.....	.....	.....
1863-64	2,432	.....	.....	.....	.....	.....	.....	2,000	3,000	1,000	.....	.....	.....	.....	.....	.....	.....	.....
1864-65	32,000	.....	.....	.....	.....	.....	.....	14,700	15,000	1,019	.....	.....	.....	.....	.....	.....	.....	.....
1865-66	39,000	.....	1,200	.....	.....	.....	.....	4,500	11,300	.....	.....	.....	.....	.....	.....	.....	.....	.....
1866-67	55,000	.....	.....	.....	.....	.....	.....	7,000	28,000	2,000	.....	.....	.....	.....	.....	.....	.....	.....
1867-68	105,000	.....	3,400	.....	1,600	.....	.....	25,701	54,000	5,000	.....	.....	.....	5,000	15,000	.....	.....	.....
1868-69	40,000	.....	.....	.....	.....	.....	.....	.....	.....	.....	.....	.....	.....	5,000	5,945	.....	.....	.....
1869-70	49,048	.....	.....	.....	.....	.....	.....	18,297	78,433	.....	.....	.....	.....	14,100	19,310	899	.....	.....
1870-71	.....	.....	.....	.....	.....	.....	.....	.....	.....	.....	.....	.....	.....	.....	.....	.....	.....	.....
1871-72	.....	.....	.....	.....	800	.....	.....	700	.....	.....	.....	.....	.....	.....	.....	.....	.....	.....
1872-73	1,000	.....	.....	.....	500	.....	.....	4,961	.....	.....	7,394	.....	.....	.....	.....	.....	.....	.....
1873-74	.....	.....	.....	.....	.....	.....	.....	15,743	.....	.....	4,686	.....	.....	.....	.....	.....	.....	.....
Total	337,830	500	4,600	100	2,950	378	287·25	93,602	199,783	9,019	12,080	396	243	24,100	40,255	899	75	40·28

APPENDIX C—(concluded.)

Report on the number, distribution, and condition of plants in the Government Cinchona Plantations on the Nilgiris for the half-year ending 31st July 1875.

(From Proceedings of the Madras Government, Revenue Department, dated 2nd October 1875.)

No. of species.	Botanical Names.	Commercial Names.	Number of plants.	Value per lb. of dry Bark in the London Market.*
				s. d. s. d.
1	C. succirubra	Red Bark	1,215,963	2 6 to 8 9
2	„ Calisaya	Yellow Bark	54,881	2 1 „ 9 0
3	„ *var.* frutex			
	„ *var.* vera			
	„ officinalis			
	„ *var.* Condaminia	Original Loxa Bark	1,183,159	2 10 „ 7 0
	„ *var.* Bonplandiana	Select Crown Bark	87,509	2 10 „ 7 0
	„ *var.* crispa	Fine Crown Bark	4,355	2 10 „ 5 6
4	„ lancifolia	Pitayo Bark	279	1 8 „ 2 9
5	„ nitida	Genuine Grey Bark	2,786	1 8 „ 2 10
6	„ species without name	Fine Grey Bark	8,500	1 8 „ 2 10
7	„ micrantha	Grey Bark	46,730	1 8 „ 2 9
8	„ Peruviana	Finest Grey Bark	3,389	1 8 „ 2 10
9	„ Pahudiana	Unknown	425	Unknown.
10	„ lanceolate leaved variety of C. officinalis	Ditto	23,075	Ditto.
11	„ Pitayo, raised from imported seed	Ditto	28,296	Ditto.
12	„ plants brought out by Dr. Simpson	Ditto	76	Ditto.
		TOTAL	2,659,423	

* These prices are quoted from the Nilgiri report; they do not harmonise with the prices actually ruling at recent bark sales in London as given in Appendix G, pp. 89 to 93.

OOTACAMUND, 15th June 1874.

W. G. McIVOR

Supdt. Govt. Cinchona Plantations.

APPENDIX D.

Statement of Expenditure, 1860 to 1874, of the Government Cinchona Plantations on the Nilgiris.

Particulars.	Superintendent and Office Establishment.		Propagation and Nursery Department.		Dodabetta Plantations.		Neddivuttum Plantation.		Pykara Plantation.		Maicoonbab Plantations.		Total.
	1860 to 1872-73.	1873-74.	1861 to 1872-73.	1873-74.	1860 to 1872-73.	1873-74.	1861 to 1872-73.	1873-74.	1863 to 1872-73.	1873-74.	1863 to 1872-73.	1873-74.	
	Rs.	Rs.	Rs.	Rs.	Rs.	Rs.	Rs.	Rs.	Rs.	Rs.	Rs.	Rs.	Rs.
Establishment, salaries, &c.	89,327	8,247	40,637	240	44,336	1,980	87,907	2,532	14,516	950	9,605	...	3,00,177
Buildings	185	380	14,261	...	20,816	...	23,345	461	3,636	147	3,138	...	66,369
Tool and Store-rooms	...	...	...	...	675	...	1,618	...	893	...	320	...	3,506
Coolies' quarters	...	...	...	...	1,743	...	4,298	...	2,257	40	545	...	8,883
Felling	...	...	...	...	4,568	...	9,227	...	7,576	28	4,952	...	26,351
Clearing and weeding	...	...	1,459	...	22,019	1,650	33,113	1,292	21,397	1,821	11,191	...	93,942
Pitting	...	...	...	...	9,720	76	15,725	55	6,826	354	4,623	...	37,379
Carriage of plants	...	...	...	...	3,427	...	5,048	...	1,823	...	786	...	11,084
Planting and shading	...	...	...	...	6,934	230	7,419	352	2,222	262	1,117	...	18,536
Trenching	...	...	...	...	3,759	...	6,642	...	2,065	...	575	...	13,041
Enclosing	...	...	548	...	5,337	...	4,552	...	1,845	...	1,080	...	13,362
Road-making	...	...	...	...	7,249	115	5,955	212	3,541	193	2,371	...	19,636
Tools	...	130	759	120	5,301	61	6,292	95	4,105	75	1,981	...	18,669
Contingencies	1,026	...	2,560	...	6,052	85	7,989	70	2,016	50	1,104	...	21,202
Excavating	...	...	172	...	1,094	...	1,219	...	...	...	...	...	2,289
Clothing	201	30	365	...	250	...	381	20	158	45	85	...	1,334
Various	...	...	...	525	2,795	1,064	3,508	682	840	595	303	...	10,114
Collection of bark and mossing	...	...	...	...	272	...	3,460	2,000	1,025	148	...	...	7,352
Carriage of ditto	...	...	...	...	...	...	762	100	49	...	...	...	1,059
Manure and manuring trees	...	...	...	...	40	670	28	...	3	...	...	...	741
Total	90,739	8,787	60,761	885	1,46,387	5,931	2,28,398	7,871	76,793	4,708	43,776	...	6,75,026

The expenditure on account of the Quinologist is not included in the above statement.

APPENDIX E.

Government Cinchona Plantations in British Sikkim—Stock and Area on 30th April 1875.

Years of planting	Succirubra			Calisaya			Officinalis			Micrantha			Pahudiana			New variety			Total number planted in each year	Total number of acres planted in each year
	Number plant-ed.	Distance apart, in feet.	Area in acres.	Number plant-ed.	Distance apart, in feet.	Area in acres.	Number plant-ed.	Distance apart, in feet.	Area in acres.	Number plant-ed.	Distance apart, in feet.	Area in acres.	Number plant-ed.	Distance apart, in feet.	Area in acres.	Number plant-ed.	Distance apart, in feet.	Area in acres.		
1864	389	6×6	0·321	...	...	...	...	...	...	...	...	...	...	...	...	...	...	...	389	0·321
1865	...	...	...	...	...	...	870	6×6	0·719	15	6×6	0·001	2,162	6×6	1·786	...	...	...	3,047	2·506
1866	30,998	6×6	25·618	3	...	...	29,770	5×6	17·088	143	6×6	0·118	2,930	6×6	2·421	...	...	...	63,844	45·245
1867	224,756	6×6	186·724	147	6×6	0·121	100,279	5×5	57·665	5,400	6×6	4·144	...	...	...	...	...	...	330,582	247·854
1868	320,476	6×6	265·855	70	6×6	0·057	181,800	5×5	104·361	24,109	6×6	19·324	...	...	...	...	...	...	526,464	389·197
1869	435,462	6×6	351·639	2,110	5×5	1·210	84,180	4×3	26·069	...	...	...	...	...	...	...	...	...	521,772	378·517
1870	217,615	6×8	179·847	22,530	6×6	18·619	33,101	4×3	9·118	...	...	...	...	...	...	...	...	...	273,246	207·584
1871	161,000	6×6	133·057	50,140	6×8	41·438	...	...	...	...	...	...	...	...	...	...	...	...	211,140	174·495
1872	419,295	4×4	164·097	72,500	4×4	26·629	...	...	...	...	...	...	...	...	...	...	...	...	491,795	190·636
1873	235,000	4×4	86·317	147,000	4×4	53·994	25,000	3×3	5·165	16,000	4×4	5·876	...	...	...	6,000	4×4	2·203	429,000	153·555
1874	265,000	4×4	97·337	60,000	4×4,	22·038	...	...	...	4,333	4×4	1·691	...	...	...	15,000	4×4	5·509	344,333	126·575
1875 (to 31st March)	90,000	4×4	33·057	...	...	...	...	...	...	...	...	...	...	...	...	...	...	...	90,000	33·057
TOTALS	2,390,000	...	1511·778	354,500	...	164·106	465,000	...	218·885	50,000	...	31·954	5,092	...	4·207	21,000	...	7·712	3,285,502	1939·442

The above return refers only to trees planted out, nursery stock being excluded.

APPENDICES. 89

APPENDIX F.

Revenue and Expenditure of Government Cinchona Plantations in British Sikkim, on all accounts, from their commencement to 31st March 1875.

Year.	Revenue.	Charges.
	Rs.	Rs.
1862-63	nil	9,455
1863-64	nil	10,421
1864-65	nil	39,096
1865-66	nil	59,063
1866-67	nil	48,964
*1867-68	1,068	67,601
1868-69	543	75,965
1869-70	156	54,542
1870-71	nil	54,756
1871-72	1,484	60,023
1872-73	2,320	50,795
1873-74	2,387	55,620
1874-75	nil	59,942
TOTAL	7,958	6,46,243

APPENDIX G.
PARTICULARS OF BARK SALES AT LONDON.
(The prices are per pound avoirdupois.)

21st and 26th January 1875.

91 Serons Calisaya, flat, middling to good, 2s. 6d. to 3s. 5d., about 20 sold.
405 Packages Calisaya, quill, middling to good—
        215 packages sold, 2s. 6d. to 3s. 8d.
        190   do.   bought in, 2s. to 2s. 3d.
38 Serons Caravaya, quill, fair, 1s. 9d., bought in.
1,659 Bales soft Columbian, middling to good—
        485 bales sold, 1s. 5d. to 2s.
      1,174 „ bought in, 1s. 6d. to 2s. 4d.
52 Bales New Granadian, fair, 2s. 6d., bought in.
136 Bags Maracaibo, fair, 2½d., sold.
39 Bales Carthagena, middling, hard, 1s. 1d. to 1s. 2d., sold.
46 „ Ceylon Cinchona, middling to fair, 8d. to 1s. 8d., sold.
420 „ Ashy Crown—
        21 bales, fair to good, 1s. 6d. to 2s. 4d., sold.
        399 „ ordinary to fair, 3d. to 1s. 1d., sold.
169 Sacks Mossy Lima, fair to good, 3d. to 4d., sold.
34 Serons Crown, very ordinary to middling, 4d. to 1s. 5d., sold.
67 Bales Red, fair to good, but rather small, 1s. to 2s., about three-fourths sold.

4th and 9th February 1875.

492 Serons Calisaya, quill, middling to good, 2s. 6d. to 3s. 5d., about 320 sold.
40 Ditto ditto   common, smooth like Crown, withdrawn
85 Ditto ditto   „   1s. to 2s., about 60 sold, 1s. 4d. to 1s. 6d.

3 Serons Calisaya, bold quill, fair to good, 3s. 4d. to 3s. 11d., sold.
 76 Ditto   ditto, flat, middling to good, 2s. 6d. to 3s. 3d., about 20 sold, 3s. to 3s. 3d.
831 Ditto soft Columbian, middling to good—
     582 Serons bought in, 1s. 8d. to 2s. 8d.
     249 Ditto common, sold, 3d. to 1s. 3d.
101 Ditto New Granadian, fair, 52 Serons sold before the sale, remainder, 2s. 3d., bought in.
 37 Ditto Hard Pitayo, withdrawn.
 17 Bags Ceylon Cinchona, small, twiggy to fair, 6d. to 1s. 5d., sold.
 98 Bales Crown—
     42 Bales, fair to good, 1s. to 2s. 3d., } sold.
     36 Ditto, very ordinary, 2d. to 9d.,
 35 Ditto red, very ordinary to middling, 6d. to 1s. 3d., part sold.
 12 Serons Condurango, good, 3d., bought in.

18th and 23rd February 1875.

262 Serons Calisaya, flat, middling to fair, 2s. 2d. to 3s. 3d., about 100 sold, 2s. 9d. to 3s. 3d.
 82 Serons Calisaya, flat, ordinary to fair, all damaged, 1s. 3d. to 3s. 1d., about 50 sold.
205 Ditto   ditto,   quill, very middling to fair, 2s. 6d. to 3s., about 30 sold, 2s. 9d.
 54 Ditto   ditto,   quill, very inferior, smooth, 1s. 7d. to 2s., bought in.
  3 Ditto   ditto,   bold, picked quill, 4s. 6d. to 5s. 5d., sold.
850 Packages soft Columbian, middling to good, 1s. 5d. to 2s. 8d., about 70 sold, 1s. 9d. to 2s. 2d.
412 Packages soft Columbian, very ordinary, 1s., about 20 sold.
417 Ditto   New Granadian, middling to fair, 1s. 7d. to 2s. 8d., about 140 sold.
 32 Bales Carthagena, middling to fair, 1s. 1d. to 1s. 6d., sold.
 30 Ditto   ditto,   common, 3d. to 8d., sold.
 64 Ditto   Crown,   middling to good, 1s. to 2s. 3d., all sold.
180 Ditto   ditto,   very ordinary to middling, 3d. to 9d., about 60 sold.
267 Ditto Mossy Lima, fair to good, 4d. to 6d., bought in.
 56 Ditto Maracailes, middling to fair, 1¼d. to 3½d., sold.
 40 Ditto Red, middling to fair, 1s. to 3s. 9d., about 30 sold.
  6 Ditto Ceylon Cinchona, fair silvery quill, 1s. 7d., sold.

18th and 23rd March 1875.

 51 Serons Calisaya, flat, middling to fair, 2s. to 3s., bought in.
309   Ditto,   quill, middling to fine, 2s. to 4s. 1d., about 150 sold at 3s. 3d. to 4s. 1d.
1,693 Bales soft Columbian, middling to good—
     44 sold before the sale.
     367 withdrawn.
     303 sold, 1s. to 2s. 5d.
     979 bought in, 1s. to 2s. 8d.
183 Bales New Granadian, fair to good, 2s. to 2s. 8d., about 70 sold at 2s. 7d. to 2s. 8d.
 25   „   Hard Carthagena, 1s., bought in.
 87   „   Maracaibo, middling to fair, 2½d. to 6d., about half sold at 2½d.
 85 Serons Crown, fair to fine, 1s. 2d. to 2s. 2d., nearly all sold.
 48   „   very ordinary, 4d. to 6d., sold.
 26 Cases Red, middling to good, 1s. 6d. to 3s. 9d., about 20 sold at 1s. 6d. to 2s.
 23 Bales East India Cinchona at Madras, good to fine Officinalis, 2s. 10d. to 3s. 10d., all sold.

8th and 13th April 1875.

167 Serons Calisaya, middling, flat, 2s. 1d. to 2s. 10d., bought in.
 36   „   „   „   withdrawn.
 10   „   „   quill, 1 seron fine, sold at 3s. 5d.; remainder, middling to fair, bought in at 1s. 9d. to 2s. 10d.

APPENDICES.

126 Bales Carthagena, fair to good, 1s. 3d. to 1s. 6d., sold.
39 „ „ middling, 8d., sold.
180 Cases East India Cinchona, fair to fine, 1s. 8d. to 3s. 3d., about half sold.
907 Bales soft Columbian, middling to good—
    62 Bales withdrawn.
    845 „ 1s. to 2s. 9d., about 80 sold at 1s. to 2s. 7d.
18 Serons Hard Pitayo, fine, 2s. 5d. to 2s. 6d., bought in.
37 Cases Red, middling quilly to good flat, 1s. to 2s. 10d., about three-fourths sold.
20 Bales Maracaibo, fair, 2½d., sold.
165 Serons Crown and Grey, middling to fine, 6d. to 2s. 5d., all sold.
233 Sacks Mossy Lima, middling, 2½d. to 2¼d., about three-fourths sold.

22nd and 27th April 1875.

115 Serons Calisaya, flat, middling to fair, 2s. 6d. to 2s. 10d., about three-fourths sold.
160 Serons Calisaya, quill, middling to good, 2s. 3d. to 3s. 7d., about 100 sold.
23 „ „ „ very inferior, 1s. 7d. to 2s., bought in.
506 Bales soft Columbian, very middling to fair, 1s. to 2s. 3d., nearly all bought in.
66 „ „ very ordinary, 6d., bought in.
359 „ New Granadian, fair to good, 1s. 9d. to 2s. 9d., about 220 sold at 2s. 8d. to 2s. 9d.
51 Bales Hard Pitayo, middling, 8d. to 1s., bought in.
87 „ very ordinary Columbian, 2d., bought in.
220 Bags East India Cinchona at Madras, fair to fine, 1s. 6d. to 3s. 5d., all sold, about 97 lbs. each.
60 Cases East India Cinchona at Calicut, fair, 1s. 9d. to 2s. 1d., bought in, about 100lbs. each.
35 Serons Crown, fair to good, 1s. 3d. to 2s. 4d., sold.
22 „ „ very ordinary to middling, 4d. to 10d., bought in.
15 Cases Red, middling to fair, 2s. 4d. to 3s., bought in.
11 Bales „ fair, badly damaged, 3½d. to 4½d., sold.

1st and 6th July 1875.

72 Serons Calisaya, flat, middling to fair, 2s. 4d. to 3s. 2d., sold.
384 „ „ quill, middling to fine, 3s. to 3s. 11d., about 100 sold.
10 „ „ picked quill, 4s. 8d. to 6s. 2d., sold.
54 „ „ very inferior smooth quill, 1s. 2d. to 2s. 3d., about 35 sold at 1s. 2d. to 1s. 4d.
1,320 Bales soft Columbian, middling to good, 1s. 10d. to 2s. 7d., bought in.
201 Bales New Granadian, good, 2s. 2d. to 2s. 6d., about 60 sold at 2s. 3d. to 2s. 6d.
200 Bales Maracaibo, fair bright, 3d. to 4d., bought in.
27 Cases East India Cinchona, 21 fair quill, 1s. 5d. to 2s. 6d., bought in, 6d., twiggy 7d., sold.
79 Cases Red, 32, fair to good, heavy flat, 1s. 6d. to 4s. 8d. } all sold.
    47, small and inferior, 4½d. to 1s.
20 Bales Ashy Crown, 1s. 6d., bought in.
10 Bales Crown, fair, 1s. 5d. to 1s, 7d., sold.
63 Sacks Mossy Lima, middling to good, 2d. to 4d., bought in.

7th and 12th October 1875.

60 Serons Calisaya, flat, middling, 2s. to 3s., bought in.
20 „ „ „ 2s. 2d. to 2s. 9d., sold.
3 „ „ „ picked, 3s. 11d. to 4s., bought in.
72 „ „ quill, ordinary to good, 2s. to 3s. 6d., bought in.
23 „ „ „ good, 3s. to 3s. 5d., sold.
9 Bales Carthagena, middling, 4d. to 8d., part sold.
204 „ Soft Columbian, good, 2s. to 2s. 4d., bought in.
9 „ „ middling, 1s. 9d. to 2s., sold.

```
 83 Bales Soft Columbian withdrawn.
 14 Bags Ceylon Cinchona Red, good, 1s. 2d. to 2s. 8d., sold.
  5   „      „        Crown, good, 4s. 6d. to 4s. 7d., sold.
 12 Bales Crown, middling, 4d. to 1s. 5d., sold.
 35   „       „       „     3d. to 1s. 9d., bought in.
 59   „    Mossy Lima, middling to fair, 3d. to 4d., bought in.
```

13th October 1875.

```
 86 Serons Calisaya, flat, middling, 2s. to 3s., bought in.
 60    „        „      „       „     2s. 2d. to 2s. 9d., sold.
  3    „        „      „   picked, 3s. 11d. to 4s., bought in.
 72    „        „      „   quill, ordinary to good, 2s. to 3s., bought in.
 23·   „        „      „        good, 3s. to 3s. 5d., sold.
  9 Bales Carthagena, middling, 4d. to 8d., part sold.
204    „   Soft Columbian, good, 2s. to 2s. 4d., bought in.
  9    „      „       „    middling, 1s. 9d. to 2s., sold.
 83    „      „       „    withdrawn.
 14 Bags Ceylon-Cinchona, Red, good, 1s. 2d. to 2s. 8d., sold.
  5   „      „         Crown, good, 4s. 6d. to 4s. 7d., sold.
 12 Bales Crown, middling, 4d. to 1s. 5d., sold.
 35   „       „       „     3d. to 1s. 9d., bought in.
```

5th and 9th November 1875.

```
 65 Serons Calisaya, flat, middling, all country damaged, 2s. to 2s. 4d., bought in.
 49    „        „      ordinary, smooth quill, 1s. 6d., bought in.
512 Bales Soft Columbian, middling to good, 1s. 8d. to 2s. 8d., bought in.
145    „       „       „    very middling, 1s. to 1s. 3d., bought in.
103    „       „       „    good, sold before the sale.
117    „   Carthagena, fair to good, 1s. 5d. to 2s. 2d., sold.
 15    „       „       „    common, 7d. to 8d., sold.
 18 Cases East India Cinchona, fair quill, at Cochin and Mangalore, 2s. 4d. to
         2s. 10d., bought in.
 35 Cases Crown & Grey, fair to fine, 1s. 3d. to 2s. 7d., all sold.
  7   „      „     „    very inferior, 3d. to 8d., bought in.
 59   „    Mossy Lima, fair to good, 4½d. to 8d., bought in.
```

2nd and 7th December 1875.

```
 20 Serons Calisaya, flat, middling, 2s. 7d. to 2s. 10d., sold.
106    „       „     quill, good, 3s. 10d. to 4s. 4d., sold.
172    „       „       „   fair, 3s. 2d. to 3s. 6d., about half sold.
  6 Cases      „       „   picked, 6s., bought in.
192 Bales Carthagena, fair to good, 1s. 6d. to 2s., sold.
  8    „       „     inferior, 8d. to 1s., sold.
 81    „   Soft Columbian, withdrawn.
489    „       „       „   middling to fair, 2s. to 2s. 6d., bought in.
 21    „   New Granadian, middling, 1s. 7d., sold.
158    „   Ceylon Cinchona, fair quill, 2s. to 2s. 5d.             ⎫
 17    „       „       „    middling, small quill, 1s. 2d. to 1s. 11d. ⎬ sold.
  5 Cases Red, middling to fair, 1s. to 2s. 0d., sold.
 22 Bales Maracaibo, fair, 3d., sold.
106    „   Mossy Lima, middling to fair, 3d. to 6d., bought in.
  5 Serons Crown, good, 1s. 11d. to 3s., sold.
 83    „       „    middling to fair, 5d. to 1s. 6d., mostly bought in.
```

13th and 18th January 1876.

```
402 Serons Calisaya, flat, ordinary to fair, sound, 2s. 6d. to 3s. ⎫ about 150 sold.
                                  damaged, 7d. to 2s. 3d.          ⎭
 26    „       ,    very ordinary, 1s. 4d., bought in.
```

APPENDICES.   93

17 Serons Calisaya, middling, 2s. 2d. to 2s. 3d., sold.
266　　„　　„　quill, middling to good, 2s. 3d. to 3s. 10d.; 70 fair to good sold at 3s. 3d. to 3s. 10d., 196 middling bought in at 2s. 3d to 3s.
139　　„　　„　inferior smooth quill, sound, 1s. to 1s. 7d. sold ; damaged at 9d. to 1s. 3d. sold.
5 Cases　　„　　picked quill, 4s. 6d. to 5s. 9d., sold.
42 Bales Carthagena, fair to good, 1s. 6d. to 2s., sold.
19　　„　　„　inferior hard, 7d. to 11d., sold.
1995　„　Soft Columbian, fair to good, 2s. 2d. to 2s. 9d., about 300 sold.
260　　„　　„　inferior, 9d. to 1s., bought in.
327　„　New Granadian, 1s. 9d. to 2s. 8d., mostly sold.
38　„　East India Cinchona, good quill, 2s. 5d. to 3s. 6d.　⎫
43　„　　„　　„　middling quill, 1s. 2d. to 1s. 11d. ⎬ sold.
55 Serons Crown, fair to fine, 1s. 5d. to 3s. 5d., all sold.
154　„　　„　ordinary to middling, 3d. to 1s. 1d., mostly bought in.
81 Bags Mossy Lima, fair to good bright, 3d. to 6d., part sold.
18 Cases Red, fair, bright quilly and flattish, 1s. 6d. to 2s. 5d., ⎫ sold.
　　pickings and dust, 7d. to 9d. ⎬
101 Bales Maracaibo Bark, 3d. to 3½d., bought in.

27th January and 1st February 1876.

131 Serons Calisaya, flat, very middling to fair, 2s. to 3s., about half sold at 2s. to 2s. 8d.
163 Serons Calisaya, quill, good to fine, 3s. 3d. to 3s. 10d., all sold.
28　　„　　„　　„　middling, 3s., bought in.
20　　„　　„　　„　ordinary, 1s. 10d., do.
49　　„　　„　　„　very ordinary, smooth-likeCrown, 1s. to 1s. 6d., bought in.
6 Cases　　„　　„　fine picked, 5s. 6d. to 5s. 10d., sold.
169 Serons Soft Columbian, fair to good, 1s. 8d. to 2s. 6d., about 40 sold at 1s. 8d. to 1s. 9d.
58 Serons Hard Pitayo, fair, 1s. 3d., sold.
6 Cases East India Cinchona Bark, middling to fair quill, ⎫ sold.
　　　　　　　　　　　　　　　　　　1s. 10d. to 2s. 3d., ⎬
58 Bales Carthagena, fair to good, 1s. 7d. to 1s. 9d., all sold.
8　„　　„　inferior hard quill, 6d., sold.
44 Serons Ashy Crown, good to fine, 2s. 1d. to 2s. 10d., all sold.
70　　„　　„　middling to fair, 1s. 1d. to 1s. 9d., all sold.
44　　„　　„　very ordinary, 6d. to 9d., bought in.
280 Bags Mossy Lima, ordinary to fair, 2d. to 4d., bought in.

24th and 29th February 1876.

48 Serons Calisaya, flat, very ordinary to middling, all damaged, 1s. to 2s., bought in.
114 Serons Calisaya, quill, very ordinary, 9d. to 1s., bought in.
20　　„　　flat, fair sound, 2s. 6d. to 2s. 8d., sold.
330　„　New Granadian, fair to good, 1s. 6d. to 3s. 2d., about 300 sold.
123　„　　„　inferior, 1s. 1d. to 1s. 7d., all sold.
470　„　Soft Columbian, ordinary to good, 1s. to 2s. 7d., bought in.
67　„　　„　sold before the sale.
37　„　Carthagena, fair to good, 1s. 7d. to 1s. 9d., all sold.
13　„　　„　very middling, 5d. to 9d., sold,
256　„　Ashy Crown, middling to fine, 1s. 5d. to 2s. 9d., all sold.
37　„　Crown, very ordinary to middling, 3d. to 1s. 3d., bought in.
11　„　Red, middling to fair, 1s. 6d. to 2s. 3d., bought in.
20　„　Mossy Lima, fair, 4d., bought in.
9 Cases East India Cinchona, fair quill, 2s. 3d. to 3s., bought in.

APPENDIX H.

Meteorological Observations made at the Botanical Gardens, Ootacamund, from 1st April 1868 to 31st March 1869.

Months.	Dry Bulb.				Wet Bulb.				Maximum in shade.	Minimum in shade.	Rainfall.			
	7 A.M.	2 P.M.	6 P.M.	Daily mean.	7 A.M.	2 P.M.	6 P.M.	Daily mean.			Inches.	Cents.	Days with rain.	Days without rain.
April 1868 . .	58·57	72·71	61·71	64·33	53·86	60·93	56·79	57·19	77·87	53·23	...	75	11	20
May ,, . .	57·0	70·36	60·96	62·77	54·20	61·48	57·32	57·67	73·77	53·93	7	09	20	11
June ,, . .	54·75	62·35	55·30	57·47	53·85	58·65	54·45	55·85	63·71	53·63	8	63	21	9
July ,, . .	53·47	61·59	54·97	56·61	52·79	59·05	53·58	55·14	...	...	10	35	23	8
August ,, . .	53·57	63·0	55·10	57·22	52·71	59·29	53·90	55·30	65·68	...	3	14	18	13
September ,, . .	52·54	64·27	56·31	57·71	51·46	59·86	55·04	55·46	67·40	...	7	59	18	12
October ,, . .	53·56	65·30	56·52	58·46	50·96	59·74	54·74	55·15	68·39	...	9	01	20	11
Novembe ,, . .	51·23	66·12	55·69	57·68	45·96	56·12	50·65	50·98	69·90	...	3	25	6	24
December ,, . .	51 81	09·24	55·52	56·86	43·38	55·95	48·76	49·36	71·07	...	...	34	3	28
January 1869 . .	51·12	68·12	55·59	58·27	43·95	57·76	50·76	50·82	71·20	...	...	44	4	27
February ,, . .	52·19	70·0	59·44	60·54	48·44	60·12	54·62	54·40	73·48	...	...	30	3	25
March ,, . .	53·52	70·67	60·31	61·50	48·29	62·29	55·33	55·30	74·04	...	2	30	11	20
Total .	...	...	...	...	...	...	...	...	...	...	52	59	158	208
Annual mean .	53·61	67·0	57·24	59·28	40·99	59·72	53·84	54·37	70·59	...	...	...	...	...

OOTACAMUND.

W. G. McIVOR,
Supdt., Govt. Cinchona Plantations.

Neddivuttum Weather Report from 1st April 1868 to 31st March 1869.

Months.	Hygrometer.		Maximum in shade.	Minimum in shade.	Rain in inches.	Days with rain.	Days without rain.
	Dry bulb.	Wet bulb.					
April 1868 . .	66	58	82	61	0·70	2	28
May ,, . .	68	58	82	62	5·80	8	23
June ,, . .	58	57	69	55	27·9	27	3
July ,, . .	57	56	59	52	18·97	30	1
August ,, . .	59	59	62	56	30 22	22	9
September ,, . .	59	58	67	53	9·17	22	8
October ,, . .	60	60	70	57	5·24	10	21
November ,, . .	60	57	70	56	2·20	7	23
December ,, . .	60	56	74	55	...	...	31
January 1869 . .	59	50	76	51	...	...	31
February ,, . .	58	53	73	54	0·4	1	27
March ,, . .	66	64	80	58	0·57	3	28

OOTACAMUND.

W. G. McIVOR,
Supdt., Govt. Cinchona Plantations.

APPENDIX H—(continued).

Meteorological Observations made at the Botanical Gardens, Ootacamund (elevation about 7,500 feet above the sea), from April 1870 to March 1871.

Months.	Dry Bulb.				Wet Bulb.				Maximum in shade.	Rainfall.		Days with rain.	Days without rain.
	7 A.M.	2 P.M.	6 P.M.	Daily mean.	7 A.M.	2 P.M.	6 P.M.	Daily mean.		Inches.	Cents.		
April 1870	56·03	73·25	62·05	63·77	49·29	61·50	56·40	55·73	75·82	1	74	6	24
May "	57·52	70·78	61·09	63·13	53·46	62·72	57·52	57·90	73·33	4	43	14	17
June "	55·91	65·43	55·91	59·08	54·21	61·82	54·91	56·98	68·82	7	23	25	5
July "	54·93	61·74	55·77	57·48	54·00	59·38	55·45	56·27	65·16	...	95	9	22
August "	53·77	63·12	55·03	57·30	52·96	60·29	53·29	55·51	66·74	2	58	9	22
September "	55·46	63·00	55·71	58·05	53·50	59·96	54·28	55·91	65·50	1	04	4	26
October "	54·78	63·00	56·28	58·02	53·35	60·42	54·92	56·23	68·35	11	73	10	21
November "	51·48	62·82	54·20	56·16	47·27	57·72	51·34	52·11	68·62	3	00	10	21
December "	51·44	65·96	53·79	57·06	43·89	53·86	48·82	48·85	70·48	1	50	4	27
January 1871	54·47	65·53	56·53	58·84	49·53	58·31	52·41	53·41	70·90	3	39	8	23
February "	54·26	69·26	62·96	62·16	49·11	59·81	56·67	55·20	72·81	1	13	2	26
March "	59·04	69·93	63·04	64·00	50·71	58·18	55·43	54·78	75·43	1	88	6	25
Total	...	...	...	...	...	...	...	...	...	40	60	107	258
Annual Mean	54·92	66·15	57·70	59·59	50·94	59·50	54·29	54·90	70·16	...	...	...	...

OotAcamund, 1st April 1871.

W. G. McIVOR,
Supdt., Govt. Cinchona Plantations.

APPENDIX H—(concluded).

Meteorological Observations from 1st April 1870 to 31st March 1871 made on the Government Cinchona Plantations at Neddivattum, elevation above sea about 5,500 feet.

MONTHS.	DRY BULB.				WET BULB.				Minimum observed during the month.	RAINFALL.		Days with rain.	Days without rain.
	7 A.M.	2 P.M.	6 P.M.	Daily mean.	7 A.M.	2 P.M.	6 P.M.	Daily mean.		Inches.	Cents.		
April 1870	60·90	79·53	67·53	69·32	56·90	64·56	60·96	60·80	54·00	...	89	2	28
May "	60·45	74·71	61·20	65·45	57·96	65·42	58·64	60·67	54·40	2	86	7	24
June "	60·33	60·33	61·00	60·55	60·33	60·00	61·06	60·46	56·00	22	73	28	2
July "	55·13	57·10	57·26	56·50	56·00	57·32	57·26	56·86	55·03	29	86	26	5
August "	56·32	57·48	57·06	56·95	56·13	56·81	56·32	56·42	55·61	25	24	23	8
September "	55·86	56·33	56·13	56·11	55·83	56·13	55·96	55·97	55·40	22	39	23	7
October "	57·19	59·36	60·93	59·16	57·16	59·10	59·10	55·12	56·77	19	44	23	8
November "	56·27	70·23	56·80	61·10	54·13	61·43	52·50	56·02	47·23	2	67	7	23
December "	58·55	72·16	67·16	65·96	55·39	54·71	53·71	54·60	49·61	...	39	2	29
January 1871	65·64	70·84	65·77	63·75	67·41	65·36	64·55	65·94	56·06	...	35	1	30
February "	66·68	68·18	61·54	65·13	61·43	67·11	64·71	64·42	55·46	...	65	3	25
March "	64·65	79·90	70·16	71·57	51·25	75·87	53·03	60·65	53·68	...	74	3	28
TOTAL	...	...	...	...	...	...	...	...	...	128	21	148	217
Annual Mean	59·75	67·18	61·88	62·63	57·48	61·98	58·15	58·94	54·10	...	...	...	...

OOTACAMUND, 1st April 1871.

W. G. McIVOR,
Supdt., Govt. Cinchona Plantations.

APPENDICES. 97

APPENDIX I.

Abstract of Meteorological Observations at Rungbee for 1866.

Months.	First Site, Altitude 5,321 feet.					Second Site, Altitude 5,000 feet.					Third Site, Altitude 4,410 feet.					Fourth Site, Altitude 3,332 feet.					Fifth Site, Altitude 2,550 feet.					Rainfall at 2nd plantation, in inches.
	Mean temperature.	Maximum temperature.	Minimum temperature.	Mean maximum.	Mean minimum.	Mean temperature.	Maximum temperature.	Mean maximum.	Minimum temperature.	Mean minimum.	Mean temperature.	Maximum temperature.	Mean maximum.	Minimum temperature.	Mean minimum.	Mean temperature.	Maximum temperature.	Mean maximum.	Minimum temperature.	Mean minimum.	Mean temperature.	Maximum temperature.	Mean maximum.	Minimum temperature.	Mean minimum.	
January	44·1	56	52·6	34	35·6	46·0	60	54·8	34	37·4	49·9	64	56·2	37	41·7	53·9	64	59·4	41	48·4	56·5	73	65·5	44	47·5	2·2
February	45·4	59	51·5	30	35·3	46·5	65	56·3	31	36·7	52·0	71	62·3	35	41·7	54·4	71	61·6	42	49·2	57·8	75	67·7	40	48·1	3·5
March	57·4	75	67·5	41	47·3	59·9	75	70·2	46	49·6	66·4	81	77·0	40	55·8	67·9	80	75·2	56	60·6	71·1	69·5	82·8	55	59·3	0·0
April	57·5	74	68·5	43	49·5	60·1	76	70·9	43	49·4	66·1	84	70·2	44	52·9	68·5	88	74·5	54	60·0	71·4	91	84·9	51	58·0	3·7
May	63·1	78	72·7	48	63·5	65·0	79	74·0	51	56·0	69·0	86	79·0	51	63·1	71·4	88	79·5	54	63·3	75·6	90	86·5	58	64·5	5·1
June	64·3	75	69·8	57	58·6	67·0	80	74·6	58	59·5	70·9	86	78·9	56	63·3	73·5	86	79·5	61	67·6	78·3	92	87·0	67	69·7	39·2
July	64·5	72	68·3	56	60·8	67·4	70	73·1	60	61·8	70·3	89	77·3	60	63·1	70·2	88	79·1	61	67·0	76·7	89	84·2	69	69·1	40·5
August	62·3	69	65·0	58	59·6	63·5	80	75·8	59	61·3	72·5	91	81·8	60	63·1	72·0	88	77·0	61	67·2	78·5	92	87·5	68	69·4	24·2
September	61·8	66	63·8	60	57·8	63·1	76	74·3	57	60·7	69·7	81	76·8	60	67·9	70·4	80	73·6	65	61·2	77·9	90	87·3	66	59·5	19·5
October	54·2	65	59·3	42	50·1	63·3	75	72·0	61	54·8	69·2	80	74·4	54	62·6	65·3	77	69·1	57	62·8	73·5	90	83·4	56	63·6	17·8
November	50·7	62	61·0	39	40·8	55·9	69·5	66·0	42	47·6	60·3	72	69·1	48	51·5	61·7	78	70·5	47	53·8	66·6	84	86·8	50	61·4	0·0
December	42·0	53	45·0	34	36·0	49·3	69	58·6	37	40·1	52·1	70	61·6	40	42·6	54·0	67	61·6	42	40·5	57·3	76	59·1	42·5	46·6	0·6
Means	55·9	65·5	62·4	44·8	48·4	59·5	73·8	68·4	47·5	51·2	63·7	79·5	72·8	49·3	54·8	65·0	79·4	71·7	53·1	59·2	70·1	85·6	80·6	55·5	59·3	105·3

G

APPENDIX I—(continued).

Abstract of Meteorological Observations at Rungbee for 1867.

Month	Second Site, Altitude 5,000 feet.					Third Site, Altitude 4,410 feet.					Fourth Site, Altitude 3,332 feet.					Fifth Site, Altitude 2,556 feet.					Rainfall at 2nd plantation, in inches.
	Mean temperature.	Maximum temperature.	Mean maximum.	Minimum temperature.	Mean minimum.	Mean temperature.	Maximum temperature.	Mean maximum.	Minimum temperature.	Mean minimum.	Mean temperature.	Maximum temperature.	Mean maximum.	Minimum temperature.	Mean minimum.	Mean temperature.	Maximum temperature.	Mean maximum.	Minimum temperature.	Mean minimum.	
January	46·43	58·	53·66	36	39·3	46·3	68	53·2	39	43·4	51·9	68·5	58·94	40	44·96	57·4	71	66·1	43	49·7	1·46
February	46·3	59·	52·26	33	39·64	45·58	62	54·44	36	42·72	56·66	69	63·34	40	50·68	59·69	78	70·46	41	46·92	1·0
March	51·9	66·	60·51	38	43·20	56·2	68	61·36	41	49·04	65·9	70	69·42	52	62·38	69·15	81	75·	56	63·30	4·1
April	57·3	73·	62·5	47	52·1	59·2	75	65·	48	53·4	66	80	71·6	59	64·4	69·4	89	80·	51	58·8	7·9
May	63·11	74	67·92	54	56·5	63·5	75	69·37	56	57·63	67·83	81	76·17	55	59·5	75·3	91	66·9	61	63·8	10·5
June	65·2	76	69·9	56	60·78	67·2	77	72·3	57	62·1	70·5	81	77·9	58	63·2	76·9	94	69·5	63	66·3	27·9
July	66·5	74	67·56	61·5	63·45	67·6	76	71·0	62	64·3	72·16	82	78·96	64	65·66	79·3	92	88·3	68	70·5	60·0
August	64·83	73	67·39	60·5	61·35	67·23	75	70·73	63	65·73	72·53	83	78·67	62	66·48	78·12	90	87·15	66	69·1	33·1
September	65·8	70	69·4	58	62·3	62·2	73	72·4	62	64·1	72·9	85	81·8	60	64·1	78·5	84	89·0	65	66·1	29·7
October	60·1	68	64·74	47	54·0	62·1	72	65·9	50	55·3	65·1	81	76·7	49	55·6	72·0	88	64·87	62	59·13	60·5
November	52·7	66	58·6	43	46·8	63·74	66	60·26	46	47·23	59·0	76	69·9	44	48·1	68·06	84·5	79·25	50	52·98	0·65
December	47·1	60	52·2	38·5	41·1	49·5	63	53·74	40·5	45·3	55·3	68	65·4	43	45·2	...	...	...	...	...	0·05
Means	57·04	69·8	62·31	47·7	51·91	59·19	70·17	64·56	50·13	53·55	64·89	77·96	72·28	52·08	57·63	71·26	86·69	81·59	56·36	60·94	183·4

APPENDIX J.
RAINFALL, CINCHONA PLANTATIONS,
British Sikkim.

Months	1872.			1873.		
	Rungbee, 3,332 feet.	Rishap, 2,000 feet.	Rungbee, 3,332 feet.	Mungpoo, 3,400 feet.	Rishap, 2,000 feet.	
	In.	In.	In.	In.	In.	
January	0·7	1·13	0·4	0·23	0·27	
February	...	...	...	...	...	
March	1·53	1·53	2·80	2·54	2·15	
April	4·8	4·67	7·90	4·75	4·84	
May	8·8	3·79	9·80	9·25	6·50	
June	29·7	27·08	25·80	18·46	15·31	
July	40·2	33·87	35·10	29·94	27·47	
August	34·8	20·14	41·85	25·62	23·90	
September	33·75	19·07	16·15	11·32	10·17	
October	11·30	9·38	...	...	...	
November	...	...	0·09	0·09	0·09	
December	...	...	...	...	...	
Total	165·55	120·61	139·89	102·20	90·70	

APPENDIX K.

Abstract of Observations taken at Langdale Estate, Lindula, Ceylon, at 4,600 feet elevation.

Months	No. of years observed	Rainfall				Shade Temperature						Exposed Thermometers						Years observed	Mean humidity of air	Years observed	Mean cloud (0–10)
		Days' rain	Total fall in inches	Most in 24 hours	Years observed	Mean maximum	Years observed	Mean minimum	Mean temperature	Highest temperature	Lowest temperature	Years observed	Mean maximum	Years observed	Mean minimum	Highest temperature	Lowest temperature				
January	6	11	3·91	2·48	5	73·2	6	58·5	64·85	80°	45°	3	106·8	2	46·0	128°	33°	3	60	3	5·4
February	6	8	2·28	1·97	5	75·9	6	55·5	65·70	81°	45·5	3	110·0	2	50·8	126°	42°	3	57	3	4·9
March	6	9	2·10	1·50	5	78·1	7	55·5	66·90	84°	46·5	3	113·8	2	49·1	125°	39°	3	54	3	3·
April	7	16	7·04	2·96	5	78·2	7	58·1	68·15	85°	46°	3	114·8	2	52·4	136°	43°	3	68	3	6·
May	7	19	6·87	2·49	5	75·7	7	60·2	67·95	83·5	50°	3	106·0	2	58·1	133°	46°	4	71	4	8·6
June	7	26	18·30	5·10	5	70·2	7	61·0	65·60	78·5	56°	4	92·1	2	58·4	118°	48°	4	51	4	8·9
July	7	28	17·32	3·77	5	68·7	7	59·9	64·30	78°	54°	4	88·0	2	57·8	120°	48°	4	82	4	8·6
August	7	24	9·52	1·50	6	70·6	7	59·9	65·25	79·5	54°	4	99·8	2	56·8	134°	48°	4	78	4	7·8
September	7	24	16·29	5·85	6	70·0	7	59·5	64·75	80°	50°	4	96·4	2	56·3	132°	46°	4	80	4	8·3
October	7	24	13·07	3·14	6	70·7	7	58·9	64·80	79°	51°	4	100·1	2	56·3	132°	46°	4	79	4	7·2
November	7	19	7·71	2·36	6	73·2	7	58·2	65·70	79°	48°	4	107·9	2	53·8	132°	46°	4	74	4	7·1
December	7	15	4·41	2·75	6	73·4	7	57·4	65·40	79°	44·5	4	108·1	2	51·7	135°	41°	4	69	4	5·9
Means, Totals, and Extremes	...	220	107·72	5·85	...	73·2°	...	58·4°	66·8°	89°	44·5°	...	103·5°	...	54·1°	136°	33°	...	71	...	6·8

APPENDIX L.

Table of Plants per acre according to planting distance.

Distances apart in feet.	Plants in one acre.
12 by 12	303
8 by 8	681
6 by 6	1,210
5 by 5	1,742
6 by 4	1,815
5 by 4	2,178
6 by 3	2,420
4 by 4	2,722
4 by 3	3,630
3½ by 3½	3,555
3 by 3	4,640

APPENDIX M.

Reports on the action of the mixed Cinchona Alkaloid supplied from the Government Cinchona Plantation, British Sikkim, by

NORMAN CHEVERS, ESQ., M.D.,
Principal, Medical College, Calcutta.

ROBERT BIRD, ESQ., M.D.,
Civil Surgeon, Howrah.

JOSEPH EWART, ESQ., M.D.,
Surgeon Superintendent, General Hospital, Calcutta.

JOHN GAY FRENCH, ESQ., M.D.,
Late Civil Surgeon, Burdwan.

DR. CHEVERS.—"It is a rule strictly observed in hospital that none but severe cases of paludal fever are admitted to my wards. It is, however, self-evident that a new remedy cannot be subjected to a perfectly convincing test in such cases as these, as its failure might fairly be attributed to the presence of organic complications which too often resist the action of quina itself. Consequently I determined to try the alkaloid in none but simple uncomplicated cases of intermittent fever. It may be mentioned here that the whole of the eighteen cases embodied in this report were those of patients suffering from quotidian intermittent fever.

"I explained my intention to Dr. McConnell, the Resident Physician, who devoted great care to the selection of simple cases in his out-patient room.

Dr. Chevers' report.

"As the type of fever is constantly on the change, I was anxious to try the experiment in cases which were as nearly as possible identical in type. I succeeded in doing this to my satisfaction—the eighteen cases fairly representing the autumnal intermittent of September to December 1874.

"They were all marked cases of fever, the highest thermometrical readings ranging from 101·2 to 106, Fahr.

"Both the alkaloid and quina were tried in several cases, which have not been tabulated on account of the existence of splenic enlargement, bowel complaint, or some other complication.

"The table[1] embodies twelve cases in which the alkaloid was used, against six in which quina was employed.

"My practice in intermittents has for many years been to give quina to adult males in full doses of 6 grains before and after every paroxysm, and in half doses of 3 grains throughout the interval.

"Having no data by which to judge the strength of the alkaloid, I made 7 grains the full dose, and 4 grains the half dose. These doses of both drugs answering well, I continued them throughout the trial. In a young patient, nine years old, I gave the alkaloid in due proportion.

"It was arranged from the first that the course of treatment in the whole of the eighteen cases should be, as nearly as possible, exactly the same. Castor-oil was used as the aperient, and *liquor ammoniæ acetatis* as the chief ingredient of the fever mixture.

"A very large experience in the treatment of quotidians and tertians in Bengal has convinced me that, *when treatment is commenced immediately*, certain fixed doses of quina are almost invariably sufficient to prevent the occurrence of the second paroxysm. The operation admits of almost as great precision as does the loading of a gun. *Thirty* grains are sufficient in a European male adult; *twenty-five* in a European woman or native man; *twenty* in a native woman. In hospital practice, however, we cannot begin to treat our cases immediately; and in proportion to the loss of time are generally the severity of the disease and the uncertainty in the action of the remedy. It will be observed that, in what I term the alkaloid cases, there had been from two to eleven paroxysms before treatment was commenced; and that in the quina cases treatment had been preceded by from one to five paroxysms.

"An intermittent fever may be said to be arrested immediately the natural temperature of the body becomes permanently re-established. In the twelve *alkaloid cases* the number of grains which had to be taken before the natural temperature was re-established were 19 (boy of 9), 19 (adult male), 21, 30, 30, 42, 46, 48, 56, 72, 83, and 117.

"In the six *quina cases* the number of grains required to produce the same effect were 30, 31, 34, 41, 41, and 42. Hence the average quantities needful were, of the alkaloid,[2] a fraction less than 45 grains; of quina, a fraction more than 36 grains. The result of my trial appears to be that the Cinchona alkaloid is a very useful antiperiodic; but, as might be expected from its composition, somewhat less powerful than pure quina. I would note the strength of quina as being one-fourth greater than that of the alkaloid.

"I observed all the cases most carefully. I noticed nothing unpleasant, or in any way to be objected to, in the operation of the alkaloid. I invariably gave it in solution. The taste appears to be nearly that of quinine."

DR. EWART.[3]—"About the middle of September, 20 ounces of 'Cinchona alkaloid,' obtained from the Government Quinologist at Rungbee, near Darjeeling, were forwarded to me by the Surgeon-General, with a request that a careful trial of it in malarious fevers should be made at the General Hospital, and the result reported for the information of Government.

Dr. Ewart's report.

---

[1] Table omitted for the sake of brevity.
[2] In this calculation I omit the case of the boy, and also that of the man who took 117 grains, his being one of rather exceptional severity. Consequently ten alkaloid cases are placed in comparison with six quina cases.
[3] An extract from the *Annual Report of the Presidency General Hospital for the year 1874.*

APPENDICES.

"The substance consisted of a mixture in the precipitated form of all the alkaloids present in the succirubra bark. The proportions of these are, according to Mr. Wood, as follows:—

Quinine	15·5 parts.
Cinchonidine	29·0 „
Cinchonine	33·5 „
Amorphous alkaloid	17·0 „
Colouring matter	5·0 „
	100 parts.

"Thus this mixed preparation is of known composition, and is chiefly constituted of three alkaloids, the antiperiodic powers of which have already been more or less authoritatively determined. On the receipt of the mixed alkaloids it was resolved to adopt the solution recommended by Mr. Wood:—

R.
Alkaloid	2 oz.
Acid: Sulph: dil. (Ph. B.)	2½ „
Water to make	20 „

to be divided into thirty-two doses, giving half a drachm of the alkaloid for each dose for an adult. It was also arranged that, in all cases where there might be any uncertainty as to the nature of the fever in which the alkaloid was to be tried, the antiperiodic treatment was to be postponed until the diagnosis could be made free from fallacy or error. Prior to this having been accomplished, the same preliminary measures were adopted, wherever they were indicated as necessary, as are frequently employed to pave the way for the administration of quinine. Among these may be mentioned the exhibition of mild aperients, refrigerants, &c., with easily digestible articles of food. When in this manner the system had been prepared for the speediest possible absorption of the drug, and the diagnosis had been accurately pronounced, full doses of the mixed alkaloid in solution were given during or near the termination of the sweating stage of intermittents when practicable, or, where this period had passed, during the intermission, to forestall and prevent a recurrence of the paroxysm. It may further be premised that the utmost care was taken never to have the mixed alkaloid administered in any case where quinine or any other antiperiodic remedy had been previously used, so that it might be shown conclusively whether the results obtained were fairly attributable to the power of the mixed alkaloid, and no other drug. I think, after careful trial,[1] there is good reason for believing that the mixed alkaloid, which has been furnished by Mr. Wood, Government Quinologist at Rungbee, is an excellent antiperiodic. The preparation is an elegant one, and so soluble that it can always be given in a convenient quantity in solution. It is tolerated with considerable ease by the stomach, becomes rapidly absorbed, and, when given in large doses, speedily produces all the symptoms of cinchonism. Unlike its representative in Madras, its composition, as given at the commencement of this report, can, I am informed by Mr. Wood, always be guaranteed with certainty I have done my best, in conversation with Mr. Wood, to impress upon him the absolute necessity of his being able always to provide a drug of a standard composition, and I am glad to find that he is fully alive to the necessity of affording such a guarantee to the medical profession in India. With such a guarantee, I am confident that the demand for the mixed alkaloid in India will, for a long time to come, far exceed the supply. In half-drachm doses the mixed alkaloid is an efficient and safe antiperiodic, and only, in my opinion, second to quinine.

"The best time to be seized for its administration in intermittent fever is during some part of the sweating stage. Failing this, ten-grain doses three times a day, during the intermission, answer admirably in a large proportion of cases. In five-grain doses, three times a day, it forms a good bitter tonic, sharpening the appetite, improving the digestion, and expediting the completion of intestinal digestion and the primary process of assimilation. I shall endeavour to introduce it into the practice of the General Hospital, both among the in and out-door patients, as I feel convinced that a preponderating majority of cases of malarious fever will be found to be perfectly manageable under treatment with the mixed Cinchona alkaloid."

---

[1] *Vide* cases in the Annual Report.

Dr. Robert Bird.—"*Mixed Cinchona Alkaloid.*—This remedy has been successfully used by me in the cure of intermittent and remittent fevers.

Dr. Bird's report.

"*Intermittent Fever.*—In the ordinary fever and ague, five grains of the alkaloid administered thrice daily, during the intermissions, has, in most instances in my hands, proved sufficient to break the disease and restore the patient.

"*Suppressed Intermittent Fever.*—This condition is very common here in Bengal, and it apparently differs from the ordinary type of the disease in not coming to the surface. There may be a sense of cold about the spine for a little while, but there is no ague; and the daily increase in the temperature is perceptible about the back and belly, rather than on the extremities and head, and is often so slight that, if not specially looked for, it may escape observation altogether. The patient is listless and irritable for an hour or two daily, but at other times he seems fairly well. His relatives cannot say he is sick, yet they admit he is not well; and he daily grows weaker and thinner, until it is suddenly discovered that the spleen and liver are enlarged, and the blood much wanting in red corpuscles. Quinine, as a rule, fails to check the return of the febrile symptoms, or to alleviate the general sickness: it is not so, however, with the cinchona alkaloid. In two cases of this condition, when quinine, arsenic, cinchona, and even Warburgh's fever tincture had failed to exercise a beneficial influence, I achieved a cure through the administration of the cinchona alkaloid. Further experience of the drug will probably shew that, in the cure of this most intractable disease, it is the most powerful remedy we at present possess.

"*Remittent Fever.*—In the management of this disease I have found the drug useful in lengthening the remissions, and I also think in lowering the temperature. But, to bring about these results, it is necessary to give the remedy in large doses—in doses say of 30 to 40 grains—and these induce such grave nervous symptoms that the physician is scarcely warranted in administering them, while he has at hand remedies which are more efficacious in a pleasanter way.

"*Hemicrania.*—In the cure or alleviation of this disease the drug in my hands has proved almost valueless, and in efficiency infinitely inferior to bromide of potassium.

"*Physiological Action.*—In most instances the drug at first causes nausea, occasionally ending in vomiting and vertigo. These symptoms are produced by doses of five to seven grains. When doses of 30 or 40 grains are administered the heart's action becomes slower and weaker, and the temperature of the skin is lowered. Even in remittent fever perspiration is promoted, and semi-stupor is induced.

"*Conclusion.*—The drug is not so easily borne by the stomach as is quinine; it cannot therefore altogether take the place of quinine. In the cure of cases of ordinary fever and ague its virtue is equal, or nearly equal, to that of quinine. In the cure of cases of suppressed fever it is superior to quinine, and, judging from a limited experience, I am inclined to say it is superior to any drug known to me. It is to be feared that its disagreeable action on the stomach excludes it from the list of useful tonics. The experiment was made on four cases of remittent fever, twenty-seven of intermittent fever, four of suppressed intermittent fever, and four of hemicrania,—and these were mostly all of a typical character."

Dr. French.—"Owing to some mistake or oversight, the medicine did not reach me until the beginning of January, at a time when the fever season in Burdwan was coming to an end, and admissions from severe malarious fever were rarely met with. Some of the drug I brought to the Police Hospital in order to try it under my own eye, and the remainder I divided out among the most active and intelligent of my assistant surgeons and native doctors, with the object of having it carefully tested.

Dr. French's report.

"In order to make my report full and clear, I beg to forward abstracts[1] of the twenty-one cases which were treated in the Burdwan Police Hospital, and where the observations were daily entered. The reports on these cases shew clearly that the alkaloid is an antiperiodic; that in most cases it is a very good substitute for Quinine; and that in some it acts just as well, and nearly as quickly as that remedy.

"If attention be first paid to the state of the bowels, no gastric irritation follows its administration in small or ordinary doses. In continued or large doses it produces head symptoms like quinine; the chief of these is giddiness.

---

[1] Omitted, as they are too long for publication.

"In mild or ordinary cases the dose ought to be about five grains every two or three hours during the intermission. For severe cases doses of ten or fifteen grains every third or fourth hour act best.

"Of the twenty-one cases, seven were mild quotidian ague, four were ordinary quotidian ague, three cases were doubtful, but most probably they were fevers of malarious origin, two were chronic quotidian, one was chronic quartan, one mild tertian, one was obstinate chronic quartan, and one was obstinate quotidian ague. In two cases there was enlargement of the spleen. Allowing for a few days' convalescence in hospital after the last attack, one case was under treatment for 21 days, one for 14 days, one for 11 days, and the remainder for periods varying from 3 to 9 days. Taking the 21 cases, the average number of days spent in hospital was only 6·57, or about the time cases remain when treated by quinine. In no case had the drug to be discontinued and quinine substituted, and in all it effected a cure—in some cases very quickly, and in others after repeated doses."

www.ingramcontent.com/pod-product-compliance
Lightning Source LLC
Chambersburg PA
CBHW022146160426
43197CB00009B/1444